MARTIN FERGUSON SMITH, OBE, is professor emeritus of Classics at Durham University. He is well known not only as a classical scholar, but also for his highly original research and writing on Rose Macaulay, Virginia Woolf, the artists Helen and Roger Fry, Mary Gordon (first female prison inspector in Britain), Dorothy L. Sayers, Katharine Tynan, and Richard Reynolds (schoolteacher of Tolkien).

MADELEINE SYMONS
SOCIAL AND PENAL REFORMER

MARTIN FERGUSON SMITH

SilverWood

Published in 2017 by SilverWood Books

SilverWood Books Ltd
14 Small Street, Bristol, BS1 1DE, United Kingdom
www.silverwoodbooks.co.uk

Copyright © Martin Ferguson Smith 2017

The right of Martin Ferguson Smith to be identified as the author of this work has been asserted in accordance with the Copyright, Designs and Patents Act 1988 Sections 77 and 78.

All rights reserved. No part of this publication may be reproduced, stored in a retrieval system, or transmitted in any form or by any means, electronic, mechanical, photocopying, recording or otherwise, without prior permission of the copyright holder.

ISBN 978-1-78132-719-7 (paperback)
ISBN 978-1-78132-748-7 (ebook)

British Library Cataloguing in Publication Data
A CIP catalogue record for this book is available from the British Library

Page design and typesetting by SilverWood Books
Printed on responsibly sourced paper

*For Ciara Barrett Smith,
with love*

Contents

	List of Illustrations	9
	Preface	11
	Acknowledgements	13
CHAPTER 1	*Parentage, Ancestry, Early Life, and Education (1895–1916)*	15
CHAPTER 2	*The Women's Trade Union Officer (1916–1926)*	34
CHAPTER 3	*Love Affair, Motherhood, Heartbreak, and Secrecy (1926–1932)*	61
CHAPTER 4	*The Reforming Juvenile Magistrate (1932–1957) and Married Woman (1940–1955)*	70
	References	100
	Index	103

List of Illustrations

1 George Todd Symons. *By kind permission of Emma Corbett.*
2 Madeleine Symons and Mary Catharine Symons, c.1907–1910. *By kind permission of Emma Corbett.*
3 Madeleine Symons with Nancy Anderson, c.1922. *By kind permission of James Deane.*
4 Madeleine Symons, c.1924. *By kind permission of Emma Corbett.*
5 Jimmy Mallon, Warden of Toynbee Hall, c.1925–1930. *By kind permission of Toynbee Hall.*
6 Madeleine Symons with Teresa Symons, late 1927 or early 1928. *By kind permission of Emma Corbett.*
7 Madeleine Symons with Teresa Symons, c.1938. *By kind permission of Emma Corbett.*
8 Dicky Symons, 1943 or 1944. *By kind permission of Emma Corbett.*
9 Madeleine Robinson (Symons) and Harold Roper Robinson, c.1954. *By kind permission of Emma Corbett.*

Preface

Madeleine Jane Symons (1895–1957) – Robinson after her marriage in 1940 – made important contributions to the women's trade union movement during and after the First World War and to the promotion of social justice and penal reform throughout her adult life. Her career as a trade union officer was ended in 1926 by happenings that were kept secret from all but her closest friends – pregnancy and motherhood outside marriage. When she returned to public life in 1932, it was as a juvenile magistrate in London. For the next twenty-five years she gave outstanding service not only to the juvenile courts, but also to the Howard League for Penal Reform and other welfare organisations and to the work of departmental committees. Very little has been written about her, and it seems appropriate to mark the sixtieth anniversary of her death with the first substantial account of her life and career.

The account is presented in the firm conviction that her tireless advocacy of women's and children's rights, her enlightened views on the treatment of offenders, and her hopes for more fairness and compassion are not merely of historical interest, but also of direct relevance to contemporary society. By no means all the battles she helped to fight have been won, and we should do well to learn from her experience and wisdom.

MFS
Isle of Foula, Shetland Islands
July 2017

Acknowledgements

I warmly thank Emma Teresa Corbett, granddaughter of Madeleine Symons, for permission to quote Madeleine's writings and for information about and photographs of her and her family. I am grateful also to the following: Clare Abbott; Jane Abram; Alan Boyd; Robin Brooke-Smith, Taylor Librarian and Archivist, Shrewsbury School; Judith Butterworth; Cambridge University Library; Victoria Chance; Chipping Campden School, formerly Grammar School; Coldstream Guards Archives; Anthony Cooper; James Deane; Sally Dowding; Durham University Library, with special thanks to Judith Walton; État civile, Sierre, Switzerland; Imperial War Museum, Lambeth; Jane Kirby, Archivist, Bedales School; Anne Logan; London School of Economics: The Women's Library and Governance, Legal and Policy Division Archives; Jonathan Mein; The National Archives, Kew; Damien Nelis; Barbara Anne Robinson; David James Roper Robinson; The Royal Geographical Society; Lucinda Ferguson Smith; Somerville College, Oxford, Archives; Stadsarchief, Antwerp; Anne Thomson,

Archivist, Newnham College, Cambridge; Toynbee Hall, its former Archivists Kate Bradley and Liz Allen, and its Heritage Learning and Participation Manager, Eleanor Sier; TUC Library Collections, London Metropolitan University, with special thanks to Jeff Howarth, Academic Liaison Librarian; University of Warwick, Modern Records Centre.

CHAPTER 1

Parentage, Ancestry, Early Life, and Education (1895–1916)

Madeleine Jane Symons was born in Camberwell, London, at her parents' home, 9 De Crespigny Park, Denmark Hill, on 28 July 1895. She was the only child of George Todd Symons (Figure 1) and Mary Catharine[1] Symons *née* Crighton (Figure 2). Both parents were Scottish, although her mother was born in England. Madeleine was probably given her middle name as a compliment to her maternal grandmother, Jane Crighton *née* Thomson (1827–1914), whose mother was also called Jane, as was Madeleine's maternal grandfather's mother.[2]

Her father, a shipbroker, came – appropriately enough for one of his future profession – from Greenock on the south bank of the River Clyde. He was born George Todd Symon on 15 November 1863 at 82 East Hamilton Street, the son of Charles Symon, an engineer, and Isabella Symon *née* Todd, daughter of George Todd, a seaman. "Symon"

1 This is the spelling on Mary's birth and marriage certificates, but later she was often "Catherine", including in her husband's and her own wills.
2 Jane ("Jeannie") Crighton *née* McKeich.

is not a mistake for "Symons" on the part of the registrar who documented George's birth. It is also on his parents' marriage certificate, in the *Post-Office Greenock Directory for 1863–1864*, and in the population registers of Antwerp, where he lived for several years from 1886. Why his surname was altered to Symons is not known. It is given thus on his marriage certificate, and his father is "Charles Symons" there.

Mary Symons was born on the south bank of another famous waterway, the River Mersey, in Tranmere, Birkenhead, on 19 December 1864. Her father, Robert Crighton (1821–1882), was then working as a shipbroker in Liverpool, but had been a sea captain of great skill and heroism, and he was to go back to sea for a short period when Mary was a young child. His most famous exploit was during a ferocious and prolonged Atlantic storm in late December 1853 and early January 1854. He was in command of the fast clipper vessel *Three Bells*, which had sailed from Glasgow for New York on 24 November with sixteen passengers and a crew of twenty-four. On New Year's Eve the crew sighted the steamship *San Francisco*, which, grossly overloaded with freight and passengers, had suffered severe damage, with failure of its engines and loss of life, and was drifting helplessly in mountainous seas. Another vessel, the *Kilby*, had rescued some of the surviving passengers, but many remained aboard the *San Francisco*. Although his own vessel was damaged, leaking, and short of supplies, Robert stood by the *San Francisco* for four days until another ship, the *Antarctic*, came on the scene and the storm abated sufficiently for the rescue of the remaining passengers and crew, about two hundred in all, to be accomplished. In America he was treated as the hero he was. He received *inter alia* the Freedom of the City of New York, a Congressional Life-saving Medal,[3] and celebration of his exploits in lines by the poets Walt Whitman[4] and John Greenleaf Whittier.[5] In contrast, in his own country his heroism received no recognition whatsoever. His life, with the dramatic story of the rescue as the centrepiece, is the subject of a recent book by Clare Abbott.[6]

Mary was the seventh of Robert and Jane Crighton's nine children and the younger of their two daughters. Three of the sons died young or very young, two of them before Robert was appointed the newly established Red Star Line's marine superintendent in Antwerp. The family moved there in January 1874, when Mary was nine. Robert died in 1882, and in 1884 Jane and Mary moved in with Mary's eldest brother, Robert Crighton junior (1854–1924), and his wife Mary Elizabeth Chapman, who had married in Antwerp in 1880 and lived there. Jane and Mary Crighton remained in Antwerp until 12 September 1887,[7] when they

---

3 The House of Representatives approved the award to Robert Crighton and other rescuers of the *San Francisco* on 24 July 1866. The measure was signed into law by President Andrew Johnson two days later, but Robert did not receive his medal until January 1869, fifteen years after the rescue.
4 "Song of Myself", original version lines 818–827 (later version lines 822–832).
5 "The Three Bells".
6 *Faithful of Days*.
7 Antwerp population registers 1880–1890.

went to England. Like his father, Robert worked for the Red Star Line. He and his family remained in Antwerp until 1907, when they too went to England, where Robert joined the shipbuilding company Harland & Wolff. He was the first manager of its Southampton works (1907–1912), and later the company's deputy chairman. Three other brothers of Mary were involved with seafaring and shipping. The eldest of them, Alexander Thomson Crighton, as the captain of a steamer of the Donaldson Line, twice showed himself to be a chip off the old block by rescuing vessels in distress and, in connection with one of the rescues, receiving an award from the Government of the United States. In the 1911 census he was described as a ship's husband. As we shall see, his life came to a tragic end. Another son, William Bell Crighton, captained vessels sailing to Australia, and a third, Alfred James Crighton, was a ship's engineer in his early twenties.

As already mentioned, George Symon(s) first appears in the Antwerp population registers in 1886. He was then in his early twenties. His profession is not recorded, but it is highly likely that he was already in the shipbroking business, although obviously very junior at this stage. Where and when he met Mary Crighton is not known, but it may well have been in Antwerp, when she was visiting and staying with her brother Robert. Anyhow, it was in Antwerp that the couple were married. The marriage was solemnised in accordance with the rites and ceremonies of the Church of England in the British consulate-general on 13 June 1891. Mary's address, 29 rue Albert (Albertstraat), may have been that of a lodging house. It was not that of Robert, who, their father being deceased, gave her away.[8] George's address, 92 Boulevard Léopold (Leopoldlei, now Belgiëlei), had been his on and off since December 1889, and it may have been that of the couple's first home together. It seems that they remained in Antwerp until 1894 or 1895, when they acquired the London home in which Madeleine was to be born in July 1895. According to the writer and Labour politician Mary ("Molly") Hamilton, Madeleine, as well as knowing France well, "had … grown up and been educated in Antwerp, and was completely at home there".[9] It is likely enough that Madeleine's parents made frequent visits to Antwerp when she was a child in connection with George's business and to visit Robert and family, but George's name was removed from the Antwerp population registers on 21 May 1897, so it looks as though Hamilton is mistaken. Her memory often lets her down, and she does not even get Madeleine's names right, calling her "Madeline Symonds".

Until at least February 1899, when George was made a Fellow of the Royal Geographical Society, the family's London address was still the one in Denmark Hill, but later that year they moved to Lenia, 28 West Hill, Wandsworth, about five miles west of Camberwell and still south of the Thames. This was their home at the time of the 1901 census, which shows that they had with them Mary's widowed

---

[8] Robert himself had married in the British consulate-general in Antwerp in 1880.
[9] Hamilton, *Remembering My Good Friends*, p. 207.

mother, Jane Crighton, and three live-in servants, including a German governess named Bertha Stroh. The Symonses did not stay long at Lenia. By now George had his own shipbroking firm, which was soon to have premises in the heart of the City of London. From 1902 or 1903 G.T. Symons & Company operated from 18 Leadenhall Street, before moving in 1910 the short distance to 4 Lloyd's Avenue. The business flourished, and, as well as being the senior partner in his own firm, George was a director of at least six other companies with interests and operations overseas. It is indicative of his and his family's prosperous circumstances that before the end of 1901 they and Jane Crighton moved to Hadley Lodge, a large and imposing Georgian mansion with a southerly aspect and fine views, at Monken Hadley near Barnet, twelve miles north of London on the border of Middlesex and Hertfordshire. From there George could easily commute to work, taking the train to Ludgate Station in the City. At that time Hadley Lodge offered several gracious reception rooms, seven main bedrooms, six servants' bedrooms, a billiard room, heated greenhouses, stables, and garages.[10] The grounds, which included a walled kitchen-garden, a paddock, and some woodland, extended to nearly nine and a half acres (3.8 hectares). George came to own a 26 hp Delaunay Belleville limousine, a luxury vehicle, which sold in Britain for about £900, the equivalent of more than £45,000 today. Such were the comfortable and indeed affluent circumstances in which Madeleine, who

10   The house was destroyed by fire in suspicious circumstances in 1981, and later rebuilt.

was to devote her life to social justice and reform, grew up and started her professional career.

From not later than 1910, and probably from 1908 or 1909, until the summer of 1913 Madeleine was a pupil at a private girls' school. Its headmistress, Elizabeth Helen Chegwyn (1860–1946) – Cox until her marriage in December 1908 – and her assistant, Laura Mary Smith (born 1856), had run a girls' school called Birklands in Hornsey Lane, Highgate, in north London.[11] Standing in grounds of about one acre, Birklands had fifteen boarders in 1901. There was no room for significant expansion, and in 1905 Cox and Smith relocated the school to New House Park, a mansion with eighty-five acres of grounds a mile and a half from St Albans, on London Road. They called the school New Birklands. Although it was only about eight miles from Hadley Lodge, Madeleine was a boarder – one of forty-three at the time of the 1911 census. The teaching was good, and there was ample provision for games, including tennis, hockey, cricket, and golf. In her last year Madeleine was Head Girl. One of her fellow pupils at Birklands was Dorothy Garrod (1892–1968). Dorothy was three years older than Madeleine, and left Birklands two years before her. She too was Head Girl. She was also the first editor of *Birklands School Magazine* and later described the difficulty she sometimes had in eliciting contributions:

---

11 The founder of the school was (Miss) Mary Anne Leighton (c.1830–1883). When she died, Elizabeth Cox, who had joined the staff in 1879, succeeded her as principal. See *Birklands School Magazine* (Easter Term 1923), p. 1.

> I remember beating Madeleine with a hair-brush to make her write. I have since learnt that this is not the most effective way of getting the best out of people.[12]

The earliest issues of the magazine do not seem to have survived, and for two years after Dorothy left Birklands in 1911 no issues of it appeared. It was revived in the Christmas Term 1913, just after Madeleine had left. So we do not have any of the contributions elicited from her by the hairbrush-wielding Dorothy, but the eleven-year run of issues (1913–1923) in the Library of the Imperial War Museum in Lambeth[13] reveals that both of them kept in close touch with the school after they left, visiting it and sending it news, and the magazine is a useful source of information about both of them, as well as about the activities, atmosphere, and ethos of a girls' boarding school just before, during, and after the First World War.[14]

Just after Madeleine left Birklands, a shocking incident rocked her whole family. On 3 August 1913 her maternal uncle Alexander Thomson Crighton shot himself dead

---

12   *Birklands School Magazine* (Autumn Term 1919), p. 8.
13   Catalogue reference E.J.1106.
14   Birklands continued in existence as a girls' boarding school until 1969, when it was acquired by Hertfordshire County Council. From 1971 to 1984 it was used as an annexe of Hatfield Polytechnic. In 1986 a development company, which had obtained permission to convert the main house into six apartments, carried out preparatory work on the project by demolishing the classroom wings, but in the evening of 4 November Birklands was gutted by what a local newspaper described as "a mystery fire". See *St Albans Review* (6 November 1986), p. 1. The site had been visited previously by children and vandals, and perhaps it was not just chance that the fire occurred on the eve of Guy Fawkes Day.

with an automatic pistol in the sleeping car of a train at St Pancras Station in London, while of "unsound mind". He was aged fifty-two and unmarried. His death will have hit Madeleine's mother and grandmother particularly hard. The latter was continuing to live at Hadley Lodge, and was to die there on 10 June 1914, aged eighty-six.

Madeleine and Dorothy went up to Newnham College, Cambridge, at the same time, in the autumn of 1913, and were both in Sidgwick Hall. They were friends throughout their three years there and later. Dorothy, who read history in Cambridge, studied anthropology in Oxford and Paris after the First World War and became an archaeologist and palaeolithic historian of great distinction. In 1939 she was elected to the Disney Chair of Archaeology at Cambridge, becoming the first woman to gain a professorial appointment at Cambridge or Oxford.

Madeleine read economics. She was sometimes said to have had a brilliant career at Cambridge, but her academic performance was moderate: in Tripos Part I, in 1915, she was placed in the third class; and in Part II, in 1916, in the second class, division two.[15] However, she played a full and lively part in extra-curricular activities. Most notably from the point of view of her career, she was a prominent participant in the Newnham College Political Debating Society and especially in the Newnham College Society for Women's Suffrage (NCSWS). Anne Logan is somewhat unsure about her identity as a feminist,

---

15   Dorothy Garrod's results were no better: in Tripos Part I she obtained an aegrotat, and in Part II she was placed in the second class, division two.

as she was probably a little too young to have been involved in women's suffrage and a fuller understanding of her viewpoint is hampered by the paucity of sources.[16]

There is certainly no record of her having been involved in the campaign for women's suffrage before she went to Cambridge, and, given her consistent reliance on reasoned argument during her adult life, one may doubt whether she would have approved of some of the actions of the suffragettes, but one may guess that at Birklands she took a sympathetic interest in women's suffrage, and there is ample evidence of her commitment to it during her time at Newnham. She was president of the NCSWS throughout her last year (1915–1916). When the suffragist Rachel ("Ray") Conn Strachey *née* Costelloe (1887–1940) spoke to the NCSWS in November 1915, Madeleine wrote the report of the meeting for the College magazine, *Thersites*.[17] Ray Strachey had been a student at Newnham in 1905–1908 and, like Elinor Rendel, had come under the influence of the suffragist Blanche Athena Clough (1861–1960), vice-principal of Newnham from 1896 to 1920. The November 1915 meeting was chaired by "B.A.", as students called her, and it is highly likely that Madeleine was influenced by her as well as by some of the visiting speakers she heard at Newnham. In her *Thersites* article she reports that Ray Strachey

16   Logan, "Feminist Criminology", p. 214. Logan is one of the few writers to have taken any significant interest in Madeleine: see also Logan, *Feminism and Criminal Justice*, where Madeleine appears under her married name, Robinson.
17   M[adeleine] J[ane] S[ymons], *Thersites* 46 (9 December 1915).

showed how the Suffrage question bears upon the whole problem of women's work, with which she is dealing as President of the London Society of the N[ational] U[nion of] W[omen's] S[uffrage] S[ocieties].

On 6 May 1916 the visiting speaker was Susan Lawrence (1871–1947), who

spoke on the position of women in industry since the beginning of the war, and urged the extension of Trade Union organisation among women.[18]

She too had been a student at Newnham, in 1895–1898, but left before completing her course. Only a few weeks after the May 1916 meeting, Madeleine completed her studies in Cambridge and took up a post in London, working alongside Lawrence, among others, as an officer in the Women's Trade Union League (WTUL).

Madeleine had made many friends at Newnham, and several of the friendships were only ended by death. One such friendship was with Marjorie Eva Powell, who was in the College in 1912–1915 and, like Madeleine, studied economics. She returned to Cambridge, as an economics lecturer and director of studies at Girton and Newnham, in 1921. By that time her surname had changed, through marriage, to Robinson. As we shall see, her husband was later to play a very important part in Madeleine's life.

18 Newnham College *Roll Letter 1916*, p. 8.

Another lifelong friendship begun in Newnham was with Jean Isabel Smith (1891–1979). Four years older than Madeleine, Jean was up from 1911 to 1915, reading classics, then medieval and modern languages. She was the younger surviving daughter of Charles Stewart Smith, a former Royal Navy officer who had entered the consular service, and his wife, Anne ("Nannie") Georgiana Smith *née* Macaulay. He had been consul in Zanzibar, then Bilbao, before being promoted consul-general in 1900, in which capacity he served in Odessa until 1913 and in Barcelona from 1913 to 1919. Jean, educated at the Godolphin School, Salisbury, where she was Head of School and Head of House to Dorothy L. Sayers, was good at sport, especially lacrosse and cricket. She was also a talented poet, who during her years in Cambridge had compositions published not only in *Thersites* and *The Cambridge Review*, but also in several publications outside the University. She was a first cousin of the writer Rose Macaulay, of whom she saw much in her student years because Rose and her parents lived just outside Cambridge, at Great Shelford. Jean was a frequent visitor to the Macaulays' house and introduced Madeleine to them. Madeleine and Rose were to become friends.

By the time Madeleine had completed her studies at Newnham, Jean was working in London as a clerk in the Labour Regulation Department of the Ministry of Munitions. The First World War opened up to women many career opportunities that had not been available to them before, and in its middle and later years many university-educated women were recruited to work in Government departments.

Jean had been so recruited early in 1916. From the autumn of 1916 until just after the end of the war, when her employment as a civil servant came to an end, she and Madeleine shared accommodation at 14a Knollys House, a block of flats that still stands in Bloomsbury on the north side of what was then called Compton Street, but is now part of Tavistock Place. Jean's mother, writing to her husband in Barcelona, describes the flat as "a nice little place" with "a good kind of charwoman who cooks the breakfast, and does the morning work, and washes up the supper things", although she is a bit concerned that there is nobody to cook Jean's (and Madeleine's) supper.[19] The Smiths were much less well off than the Symonses: Jean and her sister had five younger brothers, of whom three were on active service and two were at boarding schools, and the need to maintain a house in England as well as to pay school fees put their finances under strain. It is likely that Madeleine's parents were paying the rent for the flat, or most of it. Certainly she and Madeleine were "helped out by presents from Mrs. Symons".[20]

The flat was very conveniently situated for Madeleine's work, being close to the premises of the Women's Trade Union League at 34 Mecklenburgh Square. It was also just a few minutes' walk from Dilke House, Malet Street, which became the League's premises in the summer of 1917. After Jean left London early in 1919, Madeleine continued to live at 14a Knollys House. She retained the flat until late

---

19 Letter from A.G. Smith to C.S. Smith, 2 December 1916. Private collection (MFS). The charwoman was a Mrs Card.
20 Ibid.

1923, when it was taken over by Dorothea ("Dorothy") Jewson (1884–1964), a political and trade union activist with whom Madeleine had worked for several years. At the general election of 6 December 1923 Jewson became one of the first three women to be elected a Labour MP.[21] She lost her seat at the general election of 29 October 1924.

Knollys House was convenient also for King's Cross Station, from which Madeleine would catch the train when she was going home. When she spent a weekend at Hadley Lodge, she frequently invited Jean to accompany her, and among Jean's unpublished papers is an untitled poem composed there in September 1916 on the sights and scents of the garden and grounds. There is also an apparently unfinished poem entitled "Hadley Lodge Weekend", written in the winter of 1916–1917, which lists some of the things she will remember when she is old and East winds blow:

> *A twilight breathing snow,*
> *White fields and clear*
> *Against the sky*
> *Bare woods washed with turquoise blue,*
> *Drawn in lapis lazuli;*
> *The grey car slurring through*
> *Known roads and dear*
> *To that dear house I know;*
> *And all as still as death*
> *In the blank snow's chilly breath …*[22]

---

21 The other two were Margaret Bondfield and Susan Lawrence.
22 Papers of Jean Isabel Smith. Private collection (MFS).

From Hadley Lodge, in the evening of Sunday 1 October 1916, Madeleine, Jean, and Dorothy Garrod witnessed a dramatic event, the memory of which is likely to have remained with all three of them for the rest of their lives. This was the shooting-down of German Zeppelin L31 commanded by Heinrich Mathy, the most successful of all Zeppelin captains. The airship crashed into an oak tree in Oakmere Park, Potters Bar, only about two miles north of Hadley Lodge. None of the crew of nineteen survived. Jean records the happening in her manuscript notebook *Interdepartmental*:

> The world in general "took air-raid action". This meant searchlights: a big one like a stationary rainbow, and a lot of flighty ones. And drumming of aeroplane engines – or Zepps? and then a succession of bombs – a flash and a thump, and a flash-flash and two thumps: and the Zepp itself, caught by the searchlights and trying to shirk them: flying low, and looking fairly large – a silver wisp, very straight and swift; we could hear the engines, and the measure of the gear almost. Then flashes (starshells?)[23] – She was making along the line of the GNR[24] we thought, from Enfield way. Then suddenly, a flash close to her: and another: and another: and she took fire all along, red and smoky at first, and then

23 The starshells or flares were fired from his biplane by Second Lieutenant Wulstan Joseph Tempest of the Thirty-Ninth Home Guard Squadron. They were a signal to ground batteries to cease firing because he was closing in to attack the Zeppelin.
24 Great Northern Railway.

brilliant and all over her: and she pitched up and dived down, roaring in flames, and came in half and dropped in pieces, and reached the ground, where the whole thing flared up again, and lit the sky, and died away; and starshells, green and white, dropped and lit high up. The people cheered fiercely; and D— was sobbing by me – *de profundis* for the dying.[25] The household – cook and Kate[26] – went off to Potter's Bar in a procession that played mouth organs: and all night cars and buses and motor cycles roared and ran northwards to see the remains. We ate biscuits, and went to read ourselves to sleep, hearing more guns and seeing searchlights, and the cars ran on. Early next morning in a chilly grey drizzle the Great North Road was full of sightseers: but when you got there there were a crowd of specials[27] and soldiers, and no one could get within a quarter of a mile. Prentice, aged 17,[28] who drove us to the station, had watched it from Barnet Hill, and went straight to the spot, over someone's garden, and had found the wreckage still burning, with "dead bodies" and all.

In 1917 the Symonses invited Jean's two youngest brothers, Jim and Henry Smith, aged sixteen and fifteen and pupils at Marlborough College and Shrewsbury School

25 D is Dorothy Garrod, who had become a Roman Catholic in 1913.
26 Kate Sharp, the parlourmaid, as Mary Symons's will reveals.
27 Special constables.
28 Frank Bernard Prentice (1898–1964), of Barnet. When he drove Madeleine, Jean, and Dorothy to the station, he was four days short of his eighteenth birthday. He went on to serve in the Royal Flying Corps.

respectively, to spend the Easter holidays at Hadley Lodge, while their parents were in Barcelona. No doubt the stay would have been delightful if Jim had not come out with chickenpox and been transferred to The London Fever Hospital. About the same time Madeleine's father fell ill with jaundice and never recovered. He died of it and septicaemia at Hadley Lodge on 17 October 1917. He was a month short of his fifty-fourth birthday. His funeral took place on 20 October 1917 in the Anglican parish church of Monken Hadley, the church of St Mary the Virgin, and the interment in Christ Church Burial Ground, St Albans Road, Barnet. Nothing is known of the relationship between him and Madeleine. His will, dated 22 July 1913, at the time when Madeleine left school and was three days short of her eighteenth birthday, made careful financial provision for her as well as for his wife, and there is no reason to believe that he was anything other than a man who was devoted to his family. He clearly cared about his daughter's education and, even if he did not wholeheartedly approve of her choice of career, at least tolerated it. The net value of his personal estate, when he died, was over £59,000, the equivalent of about £3,660,000 today. The bulk of this was used to create a trust fund, whose beneficiaries were his wife and daughter.

Mary Symons died of pulmonary tuberculosis at Palace Hotel, Montana sur Randogne, a health resort in the district of Sierre, Switzerland, on Christmas Eve 1920, and was buried in Sierre on 27 December. She was fifty-six. The net value of her personal estate was £16,771 7s 11d.

Madeleine inherited all but £2,100 of this sum. Hadley Lodge was offered for sale by auction on 26 July 1921, withdrawn from the auction, probably after the reserve figure was not reached, and sold privately shortly afterwards.[29] On Madeleine's instructions, the furniture and other contents, including the Delaunay Belleville limousine and the family's bay pony, were auctioned on the premises on 12 September 1921.[30] Although she worked hard all her adult life, she never had to depend on a salary, and after the early months of 1926 all the work she did was unpaid.

In late May 1920, when Madeleine's mother was still alive and in possession of Hadley Lodge, Rose Macaulay's novel *Potterism* appeared. She allowed Jean Smith to read a proof copy while it was in the press. Jean wrote back approvingly, but raised two points, to which Rose responded as follows:

> I'm sorry about the date of the League of Nations meeting – stupid of me, because I was there, and might easily have looked it up.[31] As to the other meeting, I didn't really know there'd been only one like that. But I think the danger of Madeleine Symons or anyone who knows her thinking I meant Jane for her is remote, don't you? As a matter of fact it is, of course, the sort of detail one would carefully avoid mentioning if it had

---

29 *The Times*, 2 August 1921, p. 16.
30 Ibid. 3 September 1921, p. 16.
31 The League of Nations meeting in the Albert Hall, put in May 1919 by Macaulay, *Potterism*, p. 59, was actually on 13 June. Madeleine was not involved.

been a portrait – which is what a good many readers fail to realise always. I hope she won't mind, in this case![32]

"The other meeting" is that "of a section of the Society for Equal Citizenship" at which Jane Potter took the chair. It is described in *Potterism*, p. 84. The speakers were all female, all under thirty, and mostly university-educated. Evidently Madeleine had chaired just such a meeting.[33] One can certainly accept that Jane Potter is not a portrait of Madeleine: for one thing, Jane is a rather selfish person, which Madeleine certainly was not, but the detail to which Jean drew attention is not the only one that might have made Madeleine wonder if she had not been in Rose's mind from time to time. It may be a coincidence that Jane was Madeleine's second name. It is much less likely to be a coincidence that Jane's parents had "a lordly mansion" at Potters Bar, given that Hadley Lodge was only two miles south of Potters Bar.

---

32   Letter of 5 March [1920]; Smith, M.F., *Dearest Jean*, p. 67.
33   Graves, p. 123, names Madeleine as one of five women who served on the Committee of the National Union of Societies for Equal Citizenship (NUSEC) "at one time or another" in the first half of the 1920s. But a search of the records of the NUSEC (reference 2/NSE) in the archives of the Women's Library at the London School of Economics produced no mention of Madeleine, either as a member of the executive committee or as a subscriber or donor, between 1919 and 1939. Logan, "Feminist Criminology", p. 214, says "there is evidence that [Madeleine] was a member of the NUSEC executive in the mid-1920s", but the only source she cites is Graves.

CHAPTER 2

The Women's Trade Union Officer (1916–1926)

From the beginning of her time as a trade union officer, Madeleine worked not only for the Women's Trade Union League (WTUL), but also for the National Federation of Women Workers (NFWW).[34] The WTUL, originally called the Women's Protective and Provident League, was founded in 1874. It was a society formed to encourage trade unionism among women. The NFWW was a registered trade union, established in 1906 by Mary Reid Macarthur (1880–1921). She had been appointed secretary of the WTUL in June 1903, when she was not quite twenty-three years old, and quickly, through her enthusiasm, energy, eloquence, and flair for organisation, gave the body new vitality. But she saw that there was also the need for a national body for women workers that would give them and their representatives more clout with employers, and from small beginnings the NFWW grew into an effective and influential organisation that did much to improve the working conditions

---

34   *Birklands School Magazine* (Christmas Term 1916), p. 35.

of women before, during, and just after the First World War.[35] Mary started as president of the NFWW, but in 1908 exchanged posts with the general secretary, Gertrude Tuckwell (1861–1951). Her devoted service to the NFWW and WTUL, which continued until her death, underlines and largely explains the close links between the two bodies. Tuckwell remained a close colleague until her retirement from trade union activities in 1918. Others prominent in both organisations included Margaret Bondfield (1873–1953), Susan Lawrence, and Dorothy Jewson. Another who worked closely with Mary Macarthur was Jimmy Mallon (1874–1961), when he became secretary of the National Anti-Sweating League (NASL), an all-party pressure group. Founded in 1906, it fought a campaign that led to the passing of the Trade Boards Act 1909. Jimmy Mallon, who sat on many trade boards, joined the executive committee of the WTUL, and Mary Macarthur served on the executive committee of the NASL.

Such was the set-up which Madeleine joined as an organiser in 1916. After a few months she sent her old school a cheerful account of her work for the WTUL and NFWW:

> It is very amusing and infinitely varied, also fairly strenuous, as it involves a good deal of evening work. I am also an assessor for the Metropolitan Munitions Court. You should see me sitting in judgment on a platform at Caxton Hall! It is an impressive sight![36]

35 For a detailed history of the NFWW, see Hunt.
36 *Birklands School Magazine* (Christmas Term 1916), p. 35.

Terms of employment and rates of pay for women workers in the munitions factories were a major concern of Mary Macarthur and her colleagues. The Munitions of War Act 1915 empowered the Ministry of Munitions to exercise control over factories. Trade union rights in the munitions industry were suspended, strikes were illegal, the freedom of workers to leave their employment was restricted, wages were regulated, and labour disputes were referred to compulsory tribunals. The law applied not only to arms manufacturing, but also to many other businesses that were judged to be necessary to the war effort, including, for example, textile companies and biscuit manufacturers. Despite what the law said, strikes were frequent. Female workers were usually paid significantly less than male ones, and the WTUL and NFWW were constantly battling to improve the wages of those they represented. In a talk at Birklands on 6 December 1919 Madeleine gave a vivid account of the dreadful conditions experienced during the war by women workers at Woolwich Arsenal, the largest munitions factory in the country. One of her duties was to serve as a workers' representative on the boards there.[37] Since Jean Smith worked in the Ministry of Munitions and read many letters expressing the grievances of employers as well as employees, one can imagine her and Madeleine having interesting, instructive, and sometimes amusing exchanges of information when they met up at the end of the day's work. I say "sometimes amusing", because, although the plight of underpaid and otherwise exploited

---

37   *Birklands School Magazine* (Autumn Term 1919), pp. 5–6.

workers would not normally be a source of merriment, Jean records in *Interdepartmental* unintentionally humorous extracts from letters from employers and employees. Here are some typical examples, the first from a worker concerning a bonus stopped for lateness, the others from employers:

> ... the bulk, which are mostly women and girls, are taken good advantage of. It is principally a come-and-go crowd from the poorer districts of Aldwick, but some of us, like myself, who are perhaps a little intellectual, feel it very keenly.

> ... I do not employ woman or girls for our class of work which is rather heavy and arkward for females.

> ... your esteemed communication as above inclosing Statutory Riles and Orders 1917, No. 9.

> ... Statuary Rules and Orders ...

In the efforts to obtain better pay and conditions for women workers Madeleine from an early stage played a significant part. At a meeting of the executive committee of the WTUL on 8 November 1917 the secretary (Mary Macarthur) "reported on the excellent work Miss Symons was doing in the matter of negotiations with firms", and her proposal to invite her to join the committee was agreed.[38]

---

38 Women's Trade Union League Minute Books, HD 6079, 1911–1921. TUC Library Collections, London Metropolitan University Archives and Special Collections.

In the last year of the war and in the years that followed, Madeleine continued to work very hard in the interests of women workers, many of whom found themselves unemployed when men returned from service in the armed forces. Equal pay for equal work had been pledged by the Government, but was all too frequently not implemented. The issue was one about which the WTUL and NFWW constantly battled in their contacts not only with employers, but also with the Government, as when Mary and Madeleine gave evidence to the War Cabinet Committee on Women in Industry on 3 October 1918.[39] Madeleine did so in her capacity as head of the Negotiations Department, which was arguably the key department. Her duties were onerous: they included travelling around the country to deal with disputes, addressing meetings, collecting information, drawing up claims, and taking them to the Court of Arbitration. Those numerous groups in whose cases she was involved in 1919–1920 included laundry workers, makers of tin boxes, safety pins, perambulators, umbrellas, aerated water, and artificial flowers, and employees of Maconochie, the Aberdeen manufacturers of tinned food, including a meat-and-vegetable stew that upset the stomachs of tens of thousands of soldiers in the trenches.[40] In March 1919, when she was a member of a deputation to the Minister of Labour, she told him that in many employment exchanges women were denied an out-of-work donation (OWD), as the

---

39 *The Times*, 5 October 1918, p. 3.
40 WTUL Minute Books, HD 6079, 1911–1921, executive committee meetings held between 10 April 1919 and 10 June 1920.

unemployment benefit introduced in November 1918 was called, if they refused to accept work at absurdly low rates. By all reports, she was an extremely successful negotiator. It was estimated that of the many hundreds of claims she took to the arbitration court she won over eighty per cent.[41]

How did she manage to be so successful? The anonymous writer of an appreciation of her, published in 1921 under the heading "A Great Negotiator", highlights the following qualities that made her "an invaluable colleague", who was Mary Macarthur's "right hand":

> Her clear and subtle intellect, her sound judgment, her peculiar gift for the lucid statement of a mass of complicated facts, and her great power of work.[42]

Her preparation was so thorough that she was always in full command of the facts. She was firm, but fair and always courteous and pleasant. She had a delightful voice, and such was her gift for persuasive speaking that she was described as the "spell-binder".[43] She won the admiration and respect not only of the workers she represented, but also of many employers.

She was a member of many trade boards, including the Laundry Trade Board, which consisted of three appointed members, seventeen representatives of the employers, all but one of them male, and seventeen representatives of the work-

---

41   Horan, p. 78.
42   *The Woman Worker* 60 (March 1921), p. 6.
43   *The Daily Sketch*, 23 April 1920.

ers, most of them female.[44] Serving on this board proved to be unusually challenging. As well as sitting on individual boards, Madeleine was elected in 1921, along with Jimmy Mallon and Jack Jones MP, to join with three representatives of the Parliamentary Committee of the Trades Union Congress in drawing up a scheme for co-ordinating the work of all trade boards.[45]

To senior figures in the WTUL and NFWW Madeleine soon became not just a highly valued professional colleague, but also a personal friend. This was not least true of Mary Macarthur. In 1911 Mary married William ("Will") Crawford Anderson, chairman of the executive committee of the Independent Labour Party and in 1914–1918 MP for the Attercliffe constituency in Sheffield. Their first child, a boy, said to have been called John, was stillborn in April 1913.[46] A second child, Anne ("Nancy") Elizabeth Anderson, was born on 17 July 1915, but in February 1919 both Mary and Will succumbed to Spanish flu, and on 25 February Will died of pneumonia. At this desperately difficult and unhappy time Madeleine was one of the friends most prominent in rallying round Mary and giving her support.[47] Mary recovered from

---

44 "Laundry Trade Board: List of Members", *The Times*, 17 May 1919, p. 7.
45 "Trade Unions and Trade Boards", *The Woman Worker* 60 (March 1921), p. 7.
46 The exact date has not been ascertained. The registration of stillbirths did not begin until 1 July 1927.
47 Hamilton, *Mary Macarthur*, p. 183. See also Bondfield, p. 171, quoting the entry in her diary for the day of the funeral, 28 February: "Mary was very brave and controlled at the crematorium. We all want to help her in every way we can. She is suffering and shattered. Gertrude Tuckwell and Madeleine Symons are the best companions for her just now. The rest of us must carry on".

the flu and courageously endured the pain inflicted by Will's death, but a few months later she became seriously ill. It was found that she had stomach cancer. She had two operations to deal with the malignant growth – the first at the end of April 1920, the second six months later, but the illness was incurable, and she died on 1 January 1921. She continued working as long as she could, not just dealing with routine office business, but planning and campaigning, making speeches, and attending conferences. In the summer of 1920, as well as attending the Labour Party Conference in Scarborough in late June, she went to Geneva for the International Socialist Congress (31 July–4 August). She was accompanied by Susan Lawrence and Madeleine. The three travelled by car, probably Madeleine's. At the National Conference of Labour Women in London on 21–22 April 1920, to chair and address which Mary had postponed her first operation, to the detriment of her health, Madeleine showed that she had international as well as national concerns by moving a resolution on the economic situation of Europe. The resolution condemned the Peace Treaty as a destructive rather than constructive settlement, and demanded its revision; called upon the Allied Governments to make peace with Russia; urged the cancellation of inter-Allied indebtedness and the establishment of an international loan; and expressed horror at the spread of famine in Europe.

To Madeleine, Mary's death, although expected, was a severe personal loss as well as a professional one. Moreover, it occurred only eight days after the death of her mother, Mary Symons, in Switzerland, and five days after her burial there. Her mother's death was probably not unexpected either, but the burden of her grief at this time must have been almost overwhelming. Probably it helped that she was kept very busy. As the only child, she had sole responsibility for winding up her mother's affairs and taking care of Hadley Lodge until it could be sold; and, as a very close colleague and friend of Mary Macarthur, she had the obligation and wish to celebrate her life and achievements, to carry forward her work, and not least to help support her daughter, Nancy, who at the age of just five was now an orphan.

It is indicative of Mary's closeness to, and trust in, Madeleine that she named her as one of the three executors of her will, the other two being the elder of her two younger sisters, Jean Reid Westley, and her brother-in-law, James Anderson. She gave custody of her daughter, Nancy, to Jean, but the relationship between Jean and Nancy was a strained one, and, as she progressed through childhood, Nancy spent much time with Madeleine, to whom she was devoted, and whom she regarded as her mentor (Figure 3).[48] It was Madeleine who suggested that Nancy be educated at Bedales School, a co-educational boarding school with a non-authoritarian regime near Petersfield in Hampshire. Nancy was a boarder there from autumn 1927 to summer 1933. Possibly Madeleine in turn had been recommended Bedales by Margery Fry, a sister of the artist and art-critic Roger Fry, whose son, Julian, had attended it in 1913–1919. Margery, whom Madeleine was to

---

48 For information about the relationship between Nancy and Madeleine I am grateful to Emma Corbett (Madeleine's granddaughter) and James Deane (Nancy's son).

get to know well, was a prominent reformer. She was secretary of the Howard League for Penal Reform and had been appointed a Justice of the Peace (JP) in 1920.

Within weeks of Mary's death a memorial committee had been formed, to decide how best to honour her memory. Its members included Madeleine, Margaret Bondfield, Susan Lawrence, Jimmy Mallon, and Gertrude Tuckwell. After much consultation and discussion, it was decided to establish a Mary Macarthur Holiday Home for Working Women, and a property called The Gables at Ongar in Essex was acquired. Madeleine was a member of the Committee of Management and assistant honorary secretary. The patroness of the charity was the consort of King George V, Queen Mary, who had long taken a close and sympathetic interest in the problems of the poor and not least in women's employment and unemployment. When, as Princess of Wales, she returned from a visit to India with her husband in May 1906, she insisted on visiting the Exhibition of Sweated Industries, with which Mary Macarthur was heavily involved. During the war she and Mary Macarthur formed what to outsiders may have seemed an unlikely friendship, but it was based very much on shared values and mutual respect. Queen Mary's Needlework Guild developed into the Queen's Work for Women Fund, and this was administered by the Central Committee for Women's Employment, of which Mary Macarthur was general secretary. The two Marys' collaboration and friendship were emphasised in a warm address of welcome delivered by Gertrude Tuckwell on 26 July 1924, when the Queen visited Ongar to view the first Mary Macarthur Home and receive purses for its endowment.[49] It is very likely that, as one of Mary Macarthur's closest colleagues, Madeleine met Queen Mary during the latter years of the war. Certainly she met her during the Ongar visit. She was much involved with fund-raising for the home. She contributed to the appeal, and it is likely to have been her high reputation at her old school that accounted for a donation from the girls of Birklands, St Albans.[50]

A few weeks after the deaths of her mother and Mary Macarthur, Madeleine felt able to accept an invitation to attend one of the Thursday soirées hosted by Naomi Royde-Smith, the literary editor of the influential *Saturday Westminster Gazette*, at 44 Princes Gardens in South Kensington. We hear about it in a letter to Jean Smith from Rose Macaulay, who from late 1919 to 1921 sometimes lodged in Naomi's top-floor flat and helped to organise the gatherings:

> It was very nice having Madeleine that Thursday. It seems that she works with Grace Barker (of our establishment). She came on a rather crazy evening when we did charades and weren't being at all grown-up or intelligent – at least only Aldous Huxley, in a corner, was trying to be. I hope she'll come again sometime.[51]

49 "The Queen at Ongar: Visit to the Mary Macarthur Home", *The Times*, 28 July 1924, p. 9.
50 For full details of the Mary Macarthur Holiday Home(s), see the Mary Macarthur Holiday Trust Archive, London Metropolitan University Archives and Special Collections.
51 Letter of 9 March 1921; Smith, M.F., *Dearest Jean*, p. 84.

Naomi Royde-Smith's diary reveals that the evening of charades was that of 3 February, and that the guests included Storm Jameson, Dorothy and Reeve Brooke, and Edith and Michael Sadleir. According to Mary Hamilton,[52] Grace Barker worked during the war with Mary Macarthur and Madeleine on industrial arbitration tribunals. She also says[53] that Grace was a nurse in Vosges in 1917–1918. By "our establishment" Rose means 44 Princes Gardens. Grace occupied a flat there. Another flat was occupied by Herbert Brough Usher, the assistant editor of the *Westminster Gazette*. A member of the Labour Party, he was to serve as personal private secretary to Prime Minister Ramsay Macdonald. In 1923 Grace and he got married. The couple had three daughters, and Grace, with whom Rose remained friendly until her (Rose's) death in 1958, went on to live to 102. As we shall see, the Ushers were to give great support to Madeleine at a time when she most needed it.

Rose too was a good friend to Madeleine both in her time of trouble and later. Another writer said to have been a friend of hers is the poet Humbert Wolfe (1885–1940), who was also a brilliantly effective civil servant. From 1915 until the end of the First World War he was a controller of labour regulation in the Ministry of Munitions. He then joined the new Ministry of Labour, where his responsibilities were labour exchanges and, from 1920, international labour matters. No doubt Madeleine first encountered him, and continued to encounter him, professionally, but, according

---

52 *Remembering*, p. 138.
53 Ibid., p. 207.

to Naomi Royde-Smith, she "knew him intimately just after the war".⁵⁴ It is possible, but by no means certain, that she means that there was a romantic attachment between them at that time. Wolfe was a married man, but had a strong romantic streak in him and enjoyed the company of attractive women. That Madeleine was attractive, including in looks (Figure 4), is not in doubt.

In early February 1921, just weeks after Mary Macarthur's death, the NFWW amalgamated with the National Union of General Workers (NUGW). Margaret Bondfield became chief secretary of the NUGW's Women Workers' Section, while Madeleine was its assistant secretary and head of its Negotiations Department.⁵⁵ Soon afterwards it was agreed that the work of the WTUL should be taken over and continued by the parliamentary committee of the Trades Union Congress (TUC), with the last executive committee of the WTUL becoming the first committee of the Women's Group.⁵⁶ These developments had little effect on Madeleine's work: essentially she continued doing what she had done before the mergers.

Her work after the mergers was no less important, difficult, and exhausting than it had been before. In July 1921 it was estimated that about 700,000 women were either unemployed or working on short time. Madeleine pointed out

---

54 Letter to Viola Garvin, 20 September 1943; Trinity College Cambridge Library, catalogue reference ERM 15.173.
55 *The Times*, 3 February 1921, p. 7; *The Woman Worker* 60 (March 1921), pp. 6–7.
56 WTUL Minute Books, HD 6079, 1911–1921, executive committee meeting, 26 May [1921].

that, since most of them had exhausted their unemployment benefit, the situation was desperate and the Government needed to relieve it by funding training for domestic service.[57] Five months after Madeleine made this plea, she and Jimmy Mallon gave evidence, on behalf of the Trade Boards Advisory Council of the TUC, to Lord Cave's Committee of Inquiry into the operation of the Trade Boards Act. Both of them had abundant experience of sitting on trade boards. They urged the Committee to resist any attempt to use the present abnormal circumstances to weaken the powers of the boards, which over the years had greatly benefited not only employees, but also employers and society.[58]

Madeleine joined the Labour Party early in her trade union career, very likely in 1916, and she remained a member until her death. At the Labour Party Conference in Brighton in the summer of 1921 she was nominated for membership of the executive committee (EC). *The Woman Worker* reported[59] that in the election Susan Lawrence was returned at the head of the Women's Panel with over three million votes, while Madeleine headed the list of unsuccesful candidates with over two million votes, "which, for the first time of nomination, is an excellent poll". At the next Conference, in June 1922, she was successful, becoming at the age of twenty-six what was said to be the youngest-ever member of the EC and the first to have obtained a university degree.[60]

57 *The Times*, 14 September 1921, p. 8.
58 *The Times*, 9 February 1922, p. 7.
59 64 (July 1921), p. 4.
60 "Youngest Member of Labour Executive: Miss Madeleine Symons", *The Manchester Guardian*, 30 June 1922, p. 8. Susan Lawrence

Her service on the EC was soon interrupted. The problem was her health, and she sought to remedy it by going abroad. Passenger lists show that on 13 April 1922 she had departed from London for Gibraltar aboard the P&O SS *Malwa* (built in Greenock, her father's birthplace), and in September 1922 she set off on much more extensive and distant travels. They are mentioned in the magazine of her old school:

> Madeleine Symons, who has been overworking for some time, is taking a holiday in the South Pacific. When last "sighted" she was in Ceylon.[61]

and

> Madeleine Symons came back in March [1923] from the South Seas after six months of peaceful and detached wandering, but since then her work has engulfed her again.[62]

The magazine's brief notices can be supplemented and corrected by reference to United States alien passenger manifests.[63] These reveal that Madeleine arrived in Honolulu, Hawaii, from Yokohama, Japan, aboard the SS

studied at Newnham, but on account of her father's death left without completing her course and taking a degree.
61 *Birklands School Magazine*, Winter Term 1922, p. 13.
62 *Birklands School Magazine*, Summer Term 1923, p. 13.
63 For the information derived from passenger lists I am indebted to Clare Abbott.

Tenyo Maru on 30 December 1922. She departed Honolulu for San Francisco on 15 January 1923 in the SS *President Taft*, arriving on 27 January. She then crossed the United States, presumably by train, and sailed from New York to Southampton in the White Star Line's SS *Olympic*, arriving on 17 February. Except for the mention of Ceylon in the magazine, there is no information about places she visited on the way out to Japan, but one may speculate that they included Bombay, Singapore, Hong Kong or Manila, and Shanghai. Anyhow, her travels took her all round the world. As her next of kin for the trip she named her uncle Robert Crighton, whose company, Harland & Wolff, had built the *Olympic*. With his huge knowledge and numerous contacts, he would have been in an excellent position to advise Madeleine about her itinerary and booking arrangements.

Despite her long holiday, Madeleine had more health problems in 1923, a year in which she moved to a flat at 14 Buckingham Street, off the Strand, which was to be her home until 1927.[64] At the end of 1923 she resigned as assistant secretary of the NUGW's Women Workers' Section on the ground of ill health.[65] She also resigned from the EC of the Labour Party. However, she remained active in several areas, and much in demand. In September 1924 she was appointed a JP for the County of London. A few weeks earlier, on 25 July 1924, she received a highly

---

64 It is unlikely to be a coincidence that, when Madeleine's mother made her will in June 1919, 14 Buckingham Street was the address of its two witnesses – H.D. Littlewood-Clarke, solicitor, and Mary Henley, housekeeper.
65 *The Labour Woman* 12, 7 (July 1924), p. 110.

prestigious and important appointment as a member of the Royal Commission on Lunacy and Mental Disorder. There was just one other woman among the Commissioners, of whom there were twelve at the start and ten at the finish.

The Commission's terms of reference were:

> to inquire as regards England and Wales into the existing law and administrative machinery in connexion with the certification, detention and care of persons who are alleged to be of unsound mind;

> to consider as regards England and Wales the extent to which provision is or should be made for the treatment without certification of persons suffering from mental disorder; and to make recommendations.[66]

The Commission, whose inquiry occupied just under two years, sat for forty-two days to receive oral evidence from over one hundred witnesses, including thirteen individuals who had been inmates of mental institutions. It is not possible here even to summarise its recommendations. Suffice it to say they were thoroughly enlightened and humane, and that many of them were to be incorporated in the Mental Treatment Act 1930. Indicative of the enlightened nature of the report is the following statement in the preliminary chapter II, entitled "General Considerations of Policy":

---

66   *Report of the Royal Commission on Lunacy and Mental Disorder*, p. 1.

It has become increasingly evident to us that there is no clear line of demarcation between mental illness and physical illness. The distinction as commonly drawn is based on a difference in symptoms. In ordinary parlance a disease is described as mental if its symptoms manifest themselves predominantly in derangement of conduct, and as physical if its symptoms manifest themselves predominantly in derangement of bodily function. This classification is manifestly imperfect. A mental illness may have physical concomitants; probably it always has, though they may be difficult of detection. A physical illness on the other hand may have, and probably always has, mental concomitants. And there are many cases in which it is a question whether the physical or the mental symptoms predominate.[67]

Less than a year after the Royal Commission was formed, and while it was still taking evidence and deliberating, Madeleine was one of those appointed by the Home Secretary, Sir William Joynson-Hicks, on 17 June 1925 to form a Committee, chaired by Lord Southborough, "to consider the several systems of disinterested management of public houses".[68] It is a further indication of her considerable reputation that her services were sought once again, but this second appointment was much less interesting and worthwhile than the previous one. The Committee came

---

67 Ibid., p. 15.
68 On the composition and work of the Committee, see National Archives File HO 326/4.

to the conclusion that there was no such thing as "disinterested management"! Moreover, four of its members were obliged to resign, and, as we shall see shortly, one of these was Madeleine.

It is a remarkable thought that, although she had served as a trade union officer for nine years, been elected a member of the executive committee of a major political party, and been appointed a JP, a member of a Royal Commission, and a member of a Home Office committee, Madeleine was not eligible to vote in a parliamentary election until 28 July 1925, when she reached her thirtieth birthday. It was not until the Representation of the People (Equal Franchise) Act became law on 2 July 1928 that the voting age for women was lowered from thirty to twenty-one. The first general election in which Madeleine was eligible to vote was that of 30 May 1929, when she was nearly thirty-four.

In the autumn of 1925 Madeleine's name was in the press in connection with two very different stories. The first story was that of the prosecution of twelve prominent members or associates of the British Communist Party (BCP) on charges of conspiracy to utter and publish seditious libels, to incite others to commit breaches of the Incitement to Munity Act 1797, and to endeavour to seduce from their allegiance persons serving in His Majesty's Forces. One of the defendants was Robert ("Robin") Page Arnot (1890–1986), a founder member of the BCP and director of the Labour (formerly "Fabian") Research Department. When he appeared with others at Bow Street Police Court on 22 October and 4 November, he was granted bail in the sum of £100, with Madeleine standing surety for him. Like her father, he was born in Greenock, but that is probably just a coincidence. At the trial in the Central Criminal Court (Old Bailey) all the accused were found guilty of all three charges. Arnot was one of those sentenced to six months' imprisonment. Madeleine was never a Communist, but she was fair-minded and principled and committed to defending the rights and liberties of others, even if she did not entirely agree with them.

The second story in which Madeleine was involved was a very curious and rather entertaining one, although not at all amusing for her at the time. On 28 October 1925 *The Daily News* printed[69] a piece with the headline

WILL THORNE'S WEDDING. SURPRISE FOR HIS COLLEAGUES. MARRIED TO MISS M. SYMONS, J.P.

Occupying almost a complete column, the report describes how the previous day Thorne, a veteran trade union leader, general secretary of the National Union of General and Municipal Workers, had sent messages to meetings of the General Council of the Trade Union Congress and West Ham Town Council, informing them that he could not be present because he was getting married that morning. In neither message did he name his bride, but *The Daily News* had been informed by "a friend of Mr. Thorne" that she was "Miss Madeleine Symons, a Justice of the Peace for

---

69   On p. 7.

London, and a well-known woman trade union leader". As the article did not fail to reveal, Thorne was more than twice Madeleine's age – sixty-eight to her thirty. It was reported that the wedding had taken place in a Roman Catholic church in Hammersmith, and that the couple had gone to the Continent for their honeymoon.

One of those who read the article was Rose Macaulay, who describes her reaction in a letter to Jean Smith:

> I got a bad shock last week on reading in *The Daily News* that Madeleine Symons had married Will Thorne! The most incredible feature in the amazing case was that they were going to live at Hammersmith – I concluded Madeleine had gone insane, to be not only marrying poor old Will Thorne but to be leaving the Adelphi for Hammersmith. I was greatly relieved to see the withdrawal next day. Did you hear of the affair? It was all so very circumstantial and detailed.[70]

The retraction appeared in *The Daily News* the day after the report of the marriage.[71] Under the headline "WILL THORNE'S WEDDING. THE IDENTITY OF THE BRIDE", the paper printed a letter of complaint from Madeleine's solicitors and, in response to it, stated that it

> deeply regrets having published the statement complained of, which is recognised to be without foundation,

---

70 Smith, M.F., *Dearest Jean*, p. 137, letter of 3 November 1925.
71 *The Daily News*, 29 October 1925, p. 7.

and offers to Miss Symons the most sincere apologies for any inconvenience she has been caused.

It went on to reveal that the bride was actually Rebecca Cecilia Sinclair, aged 46, and, quickly recovering from its embarrassing gaffe, gave its readers a spirited account of her big day, the most sensational snippet of information being that she was a Conservative. The reporter of Thorne's supposed marriage to Madeleine had recalled that at a meeting a few days earlier a heckler had asked Thorne if it was true that he was engaged, or about to be engaged, to a well-known Conservative lady,[72] adding:

> There was much laughter at this sally, and Mr. Thorne himself joined in it. The heckler now has his answer.

But evidently it was the well-informed heckler who had the last laugh.

---

72 Rebecca Sinclair died the following year, leaving Thorne widowed for the third time. In 1930 he married his fourth wife, Beatrice Nellie Collins, who survived him.

Figure 1. George Todd Symons

Figure 2. Madeleine Symons and Mary Catharine Symons, c.1907–1910

Figure 3. Madeleine Symons with Nancy Anderson, c.1922

Figure 4. Madeleine Symons, c.1924

Figure 5. Jimmy Mallon, Warden of Toynbee Hall, c.1925–1930

Figure 6. Madeleine Symons with Teresa Symons, late 1927 or early 1928

Figure 7. Madeleine Symons with Teresa Symons, c.1938

Figure 8. Dicky Symons, 1943 or 1944

Figure 9. Madeleine Robinson (Symons) and Harold Roper Robinson, c.1954

CHAPTER 3

Love Affair, Motherhood, Heartbreak, and Secrecy (1926–1932)

Madeleine's resignation from Lord Southborough's Committee occurred in April 1926 "owing to ill-health". Shortly afterwards her resignation as assistant secretary of the Mary Macarthur Holiday Home for Working Women was accepted by the Home's Committee of Management. This was at its meeting on 14 May 1926.[73] If ill health was mentioned to the Committee as a reason for her resignation, that is not recorded in the minutes. The reasons she is said to have given are "that she would be out of England[74] for some time in the near future", and that "it had been found necessary to make other arrangements in regard to the clerical work in connection with the Home". It may be assumed that she also gave up her trade union work at about the same time.

Although Madeleine may have been experiencing some

---

73 Mary Macarthur Holiday Trust Archive, 001: Minute Book 1921–1942.
74 The wording allows the possibility that Madeleine intended to go to another country in the United Kingdom rather than abroad.

sickness, the real reason for her resignations was that she was pregnant. In the present day and age having a baby outside marriage is not usually a problem for a woman in British society, but in the mid-1920s the situation was very different, and Madeleine's affair and its productive outcome were hushed up, and hushed up so successfully that they appear not to have been mentioned in print until 2011, when the present author's book *Dearest Jean* revealed what occurred. Anne Logan, in a paper published in 2010, categorically states that Madeleine "had no children".[75]

In mid-May 1926 Madeleine was about three months pregnant. On 14 November she gave birth to a daughter, Teresa Mary, in a recently established, high-class maternity nursing home, run by Miss Ellen Simpson, at 27 Welbeck Street, London W.1.[76] "Mary" was no doubt chosen because it was the name of Madeleine's mother, but perhaps also because it was the name of the baby's paternal grandmother.[77]

The first we hear about Madeleine and her child is from Rose Macaulay. Writing to Jean Smith on 10 July 1927, she reports:

> I heard from Madeleine Symons, from Sheringham, asking me if I could go down there sometime before Sept: 15th to the house she has with the Ushers. I'd like

75 "Feminist Criminology", p. 214.
76 Starting in January 1926, *The Times* announced the births of many babies at 27 Welbeck Street. Today there is still a private hospital at that address, but it specialises in cosmetic surgery.
77 Mary Ann Mallon *née* O'Hare.

to visit them if I can fit it in, but don't yet know. She says her daughter laughs all the time she doesn't sleep, which sounds good. ... But I may never get there.[78]

It is not known when Madeleine went to Sheringham on the coast of Norfolk. Three weeks later Rose wrote to Jean again:

Did I tell you both Madeleine and the Ushers had asked me to go down to them in August if I could? I don't know if I can, as I go to Petersfield almost at once on getting back to London. But I'd like to see Madeleine and her daughter. Grace is a little peevish about it all – I gather she feels that it has all rather come on her, and that she and H.B.[79] are being a little compromised in the eyes of the world – Grace, of course, tho' the kindest hearted and best of friends, in action, *would* take this line about it, and would rather feel the affront to respectability (that's middle-class midlands, I fancy)[80] than any other aspect of it. But I expect she doesn't let on to Madeleine that she feels this – if she does, it must be uncomfortable for poor M. The worst of it is that she says people are saying H.B. is the father! I can hardly believe this – but still, people will and do say anything. Grace is far too loyal to tell people who it

---

78 Smith, M.F., *Dearest Jean*, p. 150.
79 Grace's husband.
80 Given that both Grace and her husband came from Yorkshire, "midlands" does not seem entirely appropriate.

really is, of course, but she wishes Madeleine would. However, as I told her, these things soon die down, and usually the less said the better. Poor Ushers – they *are* so respectable. And so kind with it. It would be so odd to feel *respectable*, wouldn't it, of all things. But so many people do.[81]

The father of Madeleine's daughter was not H.B. Usher, but Jimmy Mallon (Figure 5). Madeleine's senior by twenty years, he is shown on Teresa's birth certificate as "journalist". That description is misleading (deliberately so, no doubt), for, although he did some writing for newspapers, his real work was social reform, in which cause he was an energetic, able, and prominent campaigner throughout his adult life. From 1906 until 1954 he worked at Toynbee Hall, the universities' settlement established in East London with the aim of improving the lives of the poor, and he was its warden from 1919 on. A charming and eloquent man, with a keen sense of humour, he was as popular as he was persuasive. Madeleine came into close professional contact with him as soon as she became an official of the Women's Trade Union League in 1916. As already mentioned, he worked closely with Mary Macarthur and joined the executive committee of the WTUL. In 1916 he even had a flat at the WTUL's address, 34 Mecklenburgh Square. Both he and Madeleine sat on many trade boards during the war. After the war they continued to work closely together on trade-board business,

---

81 Letter (from Geneva), 31 July 1927; Smith, M.F., *Dearest Jean*, p. 152.

and in other fields: for example, in 1920–1921 Madeleine taught a course at Toynbee Hall on "Problems of Women's Employment", and both were involved in the discussions and decision about how to honour Mary Macarthur's memory. So their love affair developed after ten years' close acquaintance, commitment to shared objectives, and no doubt real friendship. On 10 August 1921 Jimmy had married Stella Katherine Gardiner (1889–1981). She was a daughter of Alfred George Gardiner, editor of *The Daily News* from 1902 to 1919. There had been, and were to be, no children of the marriage, which ended only with Jimmy's death in 1961.

Teresa's birth was registered by both parents on 24 December 1926. This was forty days after the birth. Then, as now, there was a requirement for births to be registered within forty-two days. With 25 December being Christmas Day, 26 December Boxing Day and a Sunday, and 27 December a public holiday (to compensate for Boxing Day falling on a Sunday), the registration business was left until the very last day. This may have been to allow as much time as possible for discussion and decision about how to manage the situation, but another possible consideration is that 24 December was Jimmy's birthday, his fifty-second, and the couple may have wanted the two events to coincide. Perhaps at this stage they were thinking of bringing up their daughter together. But this was not to happen.

In the autumn of 1927 Madeleine returned to London from Norfolk, and Rose Macaulay, who visited her on 3 November, reports to Jean Smith that she found her far from happy:

What a good invention writing books is – it keeps one's thoughts so employed. I wish Madeleine would write something – but she says she doesn't and never has. I had tea with her yesterday, and gave her your love.[82] Teresa is as fat as butter and very engaging, and rolls on the carpet like a puppy. Madeleine I thought sad, and was sorry. I think she feels it a mistake to have settled again in London, and I gathered (though she didn't say anything of that) that perhaps this was because of associations, and what is over, and missing it horribly. But of this I know nothing – only that she was rather on the edge of tears, I think, before Teresa entered. I think for one thing T. isn't a whole time job, with that efficient nurse, and that she misses her work. I wish she'd get a job. She says she is stupid now in her brain and can't concentrate. I suppose it's having been through all that. I am very sorry about her. She said that with most people she liked to seem very cheerful, and I think she does, so I shan't speak of her like this to anyone, only of course you. Life is a queer, wry business, and she's got to a bad place in it, but she'll get through it of course. She's so much pluck. No religion, of course, which is unlucky.[83]

82   In late June 1927 Jean entered Fairacres, an Anglican convent in Oxford, as a postulant. Until she left in December she was rarely allowed to write a letter, and she would certainly not have been able to visit Madeleine. Limited communication with Rose Macaulay was permitted, because Rose was seeing Jean's book of poems, *Shepherd of Souls*, through the press.

83   Letter of 4 November 1927; Smith, M.F., *Dearest Jean*, pp. 157–158.

Rose was right to predict that Madeleine would get through a difficult period. Several years were to elapse before she returned to work, but she had already taken a positive step with regard to her private life and responsibilities by adopting Teresa. Prior to the Adoption of Children Act 1926, there was no legal framework to regulate the practice of adoption in England and Wales. The Act, which was the forerunner of modern adoption law, received Royal Assent on 4 August 1926 and came into force on 1 January 1927, and Madeleine soon petitioned the High Court of Justice Chancery Division for an adoption order to be made in her favour in respect of Teresa. The order was made on 29 July 1927. Although Madeleine's closest friends, including the Ushers, Jean Smith, and Rose Macaulay, knew that she was her daughter's natural mother, she could now present herself to the wider world as Teresa's adoptive parent, which made life much easier both for her and for Teresa (Figure 6). Eighteen months later she adopted a boy under the name of Terence Richard Symons. Known to family as "Dicky", to others as "Dick", he was born on 7 February 1925 and so was about fifteen months older than Teresa. The adoption order was made on 21 January 1929, seventeen days before Dicky's fourth birthday. Although, unlike Teresa, he was not Madeleine's biological child, she adored him, and her adoration was reciprocated. Her love of children, and the reciprocation of it by them, was manifested also in her relationship with Nancy Anderson.

Clare Abbott writes of Madeleine:

> In the 1920s she was romantically involved with Dr J.J. Mallon ... The couple had one natural and one adopted child.[84]

But Jimmy Mallon was not Dicky's adoptive parent, and he and Madeleine never cohabited. According to Madeleine's granddaughter, Emma Corbett, Teresa was told that he was her father and first met him when she was about eighteen.

In 1927 Madeleine moved from Buckingham Street to 18 Pelham Crescent, London S.W.7. Situated in South Kensington, off Fulham Road and close to the Victoria and Albert Museum, Pelham Crescent is an elegant development, constructed in or about 1833 to the design of George Basevi, architect of London's Belgrave Square and the Fitzwilliam Museum, Cambridge. Number 18 was to be her address until 1956, except in 1940–1945, when she lived outside London.

Although Madeleine had a nurse for Teresa in 1927, and probably continued to employ one after Dicky joined the family, for several years she concentrated on being a mother and kept a very low public profile. When she resigned as assistant secretary of the Mary Macarthur Home on 14 May 1926, she continued to be a member of the Committee of Management, but she did not attend its meetings, and on 29 September 1927 her resignation was reluctantly accepted. On 25 May 1928 she was urged to return, but declined. Except in 1929, she made donations to the fund for the Home's Christmas party, but it was not until 1934 that she became

---

84   *Faithful of Days*, p. 130.

involved again in administrative matters. In February of that year she agreed to be honorary secretary of the Extension Fund Appeal Committee, and on 20 December 1934 she was co-opted to the Committee of Management. The appeal was for £1,500 to extend The Gables, which Queen Mary had first visited on 26 July 1924. Now, ten years later, on 21 July 1934, the Queen made a second visit, to emphasise her continuing support for the Home and to boost the fundraising effort. Thereafter Madeleine continued to make a major contribution to the welfare of the Home's guests as a member of the Committee of Management and various sub-committees. In 1938 The Gables was sold for £2,225 and another mansion, Hargrave House, Stansted, was acquired. Madeleine chaired the sub-committee charged with planning the arrangements for the opening of Hargrave House by Queen Mary on 5 April 1939 and selected the guests to have tea with her. During the Second World War, when she was living outside London, she found it difficult to attend meetings, and on 10 December 1941 the Committee of Management considered a letter in which she tendered her resignation on that ground. The Committee preferred not to accept her resignation, "especially in view of her long and happy association with the Home".[85] After the war, when she was again living in London, she returned to the Committee, and from December 1949 until her death in March 1957 she was its chairman.

---

85   Mary Macarthur Holiday Trust Archive, 001: Minute Book 1921–1942.

CHAPTER 4

The Reforming Juvenile Magistrate (1932–1957)
and Married Woman (1940–1955)

On 17 July 1931 Madeleine attended a very large gathering at the National Labour Club to celebrate Gertrude Tuckwell's seventieth birthday, which had actually been on 25 April. Afterwards she wrote an account of the occasion[86] – an account that included a summary of Gertrude's life and career and a warm appreciation of her numerous achievements, including her long service to the WTUL and NFWW. She also mentioned, *inter alia*, her becoming London's first woman JP,[87] the part she played in the development of juvenile courts, and her role as vice-president (she was later to become president) of the National Association of Probation Officers. As we have

---

86 "Gertrude Tuckwell", *The Labour Magazine* 10, 3 (July 1931), pp. 99–100. Madeleine was to write a second appreciation of Gertrude's life and work after her death: Madeleine Robinson, J.P., "Gertrude Mary Tuckwell, C.H. 1861–1951", *Labour Woman* 39, 8 (September 1951), pp. 163–164.

87 Gertrude was selected as a JP at the same time as two other women, Lady Peggy Crewe and Beatrice Webb, but she was sworn in first, on 14 January 1920 (*The Times*, 15 January 1920, p. 9). Madeleine mistakenly gives the year as 1919.

seen, Madeleine herself had been appointed a JP in 1924, and her activities, when she returned to public life in 1932, were rather similar to those of Gertrude after she retired as a trade union officer in 1918.

In 1932 Madeleine was appointed a member of the London Panel of Juvenile Court Justices, and for the next twenty-five years, which means for the rest of her life, she was a prominent figure in the administration, critical discussion, and reform of the British system of justice, especially but not only juvenile justice. She became chairman first of Caxton Hall Juvenile Court, then, from 1941, of Stamford House (West London) Juvenile Court. She was also for a while chairman of the Kensington Petty Sessions Court.

Madeleine was an active member of the Magistrates' Association and served on its executive committee from 1934 to 1936. She also gave energetic, long-term service to the Howard League for Penal Reform (HLPR). It is not known when she joined the latter body, which had started life as the Howard Association in 1866 and been renamed when it amalgamated with the Penal Reform League in 1921. She was a member of its executive committee from December 1934 until 1945 and again from 1948 to 1957. She wrote articles for its journals, *The Howard Journal of Criminal Justice* and *The Penal Reformer.* She also wrote for *Probation*, the journal of the National Association of Probation Officers.

Subjects of her articles in 1934–1935 included the inadequate provision of hostel-accommodation for young offenders in the Children and Young Persons Act 1933;[88] the deficiencies of the same Act in respect of supervision orders;[89] and suggestions for improving the working of the juvenile courts and the treatment of offenders.[90] She was always concerned to advocate sensible arrangements and sympathetic attitudes that gave offenders the best chance of education and reform. Addressing a conference attended by 300 magistrates, probation officers, and local authority officials in Oxford on 21 December 1934, she identified some of the difficulties encountered by children as arising from defective home-relationships, educational difficulties, and adolescent disturbances. In the course of her presentation, she urged magistrates to speak to parents as well as to children in simple language they could understand, going on to give an example of how *not* to speak to them:

> In a case which appeared before one of the Metropolitan Juvenile Courts on a foggy day recently, the President of the Court informed the mother of the young delinquent that he had decided to remand the case *sine die*.

---

[88] *The Howard Journal of Criminal Justice* 4, 1 (July 1934), pp. 70–72. On 24 February 1936 she was a member of a small deputation from the Magistrates' Association to the Home Office to raise various matters to do with the administration of the 1933 Act, including increased provision and use of hostels (*The Times*, 25 February 1936, p. 9).

[89] "Supervision Orders and Committal to Fit Person: Address to the Twenty-second Conference of Probation Officers", *Probation*, July 1934, pp. 311–312.

[90] "Juvenile Courts: An Address to the Lincoln Conference of the Midland Probation Officers", *Probation*, October 1934, pp. 331, 326 [*sic*].

"I know the magistrate means well and all that", said the poor woman, "but I may lose my work if I have to come back again to Court on a sunny die"![91]

When Madeleine gave the address in Oxford, she had recently[92] been appointed by the Home Secretary to serve on the Departmental Committee on the Social Services in Courts of Summary Jurisdiction. The Committee had nine members – seven men and two women. Its terms of reference were:

> to enquire into the social services connected with the administration of justice in courts of summary jurisdiction, including the supervision of persons released on probation and in suitable cases of persons ordered to pay fines; the application of conciliation methods to matrimonial disputes; and the making of social investigations on behalf of the court and other work falling or likely to fall upon probation officers; and to report on the above questions and as to what changes are required in the existing organisation of probation services and otherwise.[93]

The Committee worked hard and made rapid progress, holding forty-seven meetings, examining 126 witnesses, and signing off the report on 13 March 1936. Among its many

---

91 *Probation*, January 1935, pp. 341–342, at p. 342.
92 9 October 1934.
93 *Report of the Departmental Committee*, pp. v, vi.

recommendations, presented in 180 main sections, were the following: in matrimonial cases conciliation should be left to the discretion of the courts, and should not be a statutory requirement; matrimonial cases should be heard by no more than three Justices, one of whom should be a woman; admission to hearings should be restricted to the parties involved, and indiscriminate reporting of cases is contrary to the public interest; the probation system should no longer be organised as a voluntary service, but on a wholly public and professional basis: voluntary assistance might be useful to probation officers in individual cases, but should be strictly supervised. From one of the Committee's recommendations, Madeleine and the other woman on it, J.I. Wall of the Home Office, dissented. Their reservations concerned certain matters in section 102 (iv), sub-headed "Without proceeding to conviction".[94] Madeleine explained her reservations at some length.[95] Her concern was that the Committee's proposed amendment to the Probation of Offenders Act 1907 "would have the effect of making a conviction the necessary prelude to Probation, Dismissal or Binding-over", whereas she thought it important to preserve the principle that probation does not involve conviction. After presenting several cogent arguments for her view, she concluded:

> In the light of all these considerations it seems desirable to retain, at least for Summary Courts, one method of treatment which allows for a suspension of the

94　Ibid., pp. 73–74.
95　Ibid., pp. 146–147.

conviction and thus makes it possible for offenders who respond to probation to avoid all the disabilities, whether of a statutory character or in respect of their reputation and record, which attach to those who have been convicted in a court of law.

Madeleine's fellow-dissenter, expressing her reservation in a single sentence, suggested "the adoption of a system whereby the original charge might be dismissed, on the offender's completing satisfactorily his term on probation". The views of both dissenters were mentioned with approval by T.W.C. Marsh, Probation Officer at Westminster Police Court, in an address reported in *Probation*, January 1937.[96] Three months later the same journal carried the text of a debate on "Conviction and Probation" between A.C.C. Willway, another member of the Departmental Committee, and Madeleine, who took the opportunity to argue her case in more detail.[97]

The high regard with which Madeleine's experience and expertise in the area of probation was held is further indicated by her appointment by the Home Secretary as a member of the London Probation Committee for a period of three years from 1 January 1937.[98]

Another area in which she was much interested was

---

96 Pp. 106–107, at p. 107.
97 *Probation*, April 1937, pp. 117–120, 128. Willway is erroneously given the initials A.C.E. According to the advance notice of the meeting, in *Probation*, October 1936, p. 95, the meeting was to be on 9 February 1937, and the question to be debated was "Should Probation Be Recorded as a Conviction?".
98 Ibid., p. 126.

that of matrimonial cases. As we have seen, this had been investigated by the Departmental Committee on the Social Services. Addressing the Magistrates' Association Conference in Leicester on 6 July 1937, Madeleine said that each year about 14,000 persons had summonses heard in connection with matrimonial cases. These people were not criminals, but citizens seeking a legal remedy for their problems. She urged the appointment of more women officers, pointing out that 300 Petty Sessional divisions had no woman officer at all. At the Annual Conference of the Midland Branch of the National Association of Probation Officers in Warwick on 4 March 1937 she spoke on "A Technique for Matrimonial Cases".[99] What exactly she discussed is not known, but, given the composition of her audience, one may conjecture that the address involved the role(s) to be played by probation officers in matrimonial cases, and developed one or more of the enlightened recommendations made by the Departmental Committee on the Social Services. Significantly perhaps her membership of that Committee is mentioned in the brief notice of her talk.

In the old days, when Madeleine was a trade union officer, there were occasions when she addressed large gatherings of workers in dispute with their employers, and she was used to speaking and debating at sizeable gatherings of magistrates and probation officers. But it would be understandable if she had been somewhat apprehensive in advance of what seems to have been her début as a radio broadcaster. This

---

99   *Probation*, April 1937, p. 121.

was in the evening of Saturday, 16 October 1937, when the BBC Regional Station broadcast a fifty-minute programme entitled "Prison Reform, a Discussion on the British System". Madeleine was the only woman among the five contributors, but she was well used to putting her views at meetings at which women were greatly outnumbered by men.

Although she advocated reform of the prison system and of the administration of justice in all areas,[100] her main focus of concern continued to be juvenile offenders and the way they were handled. This concern was manifested not only in her day-to-day work in the juvenile courts, but also through the Howard League, the Magistrates' Association, her membership of numerous committees and delegations to the Home Office, and thoughtful articles[101] and speeches. In a speech to the National Association of Probation Officers on 3 May 1938 she turned her attention, as she had done on previous occasions, to the problems of girls and women in connection with hostels, homes, and lodgings.[102] Another matter that much concerned her was the availability to juvenile courts of medical and psychiatric services. She spoke about this to the fourth biennial Child Guidance Inter-Clinic Conference of the British Medical Association (BMA) in London on 27 January 1939,[103] and to a joint

---

100 See e.g. her article "Magistrates' Courts in London", *The Howard Journal of Criminal Justice* 5, 2 (January 1938), pp. 57–59.
101 See e.g. her article "The Young Offender: The Work of the Children's Branch", *The Penal Reformer* 4, 4 (April 1938), pp. 11–12.
102 For the text of her speech, see *Probation*, August 1938, pp. 25–26.
103 *The Times*, 28 January 1939, p. 14; *The British Medical Journal*, 11 February 1939, p. 277.

meeting of representatives of the Magistrates' Association and the BMA in London on 23 June 1939. Her speech to the later meeting is much more extensively reported than her speech to the earlier one.[104] She stressed the importance of medical examinations to identify conditions like epilepsy, poor eyesight, pregnancy, and gross mental deficiency. Funding for such examinations was required, and magistrates needed better training if, after taking medical advice, they were to make the right decisions. She said that some of the funding difficulties could be eased by clauses 19 and 28 of the Criminal Justice Bill, if it became law, but she added:

> a serious omission from the bill is financial provision for the medical examination and treatment of children who are not offenders but who require care and protection, or are beyond control.

Madeleine mentioned another deficiency in the Criminal Justice Bill in an address to the Howard League Conference on the Bill, held at Caxton Hall, London, on 20 January 1939. In the address, entitled "Probation: Conviction or No Conviction",[105] she took the same line as the one she had taken when she dissented from the majority view of the Departmental Committee of the Social Services, and she moved the following resolution:

---

104 See *The Times*, 24 June 1939, p. 17, and especially *The Lancet*, 1 July 1939, p. 36.
105 For the text of the address, see *The Howard Journal of Criminal Justice* 5, 3 (September 1939), pp. 190–191.

That this Conference regrets that Clauses 17 and 18 of the Criminal Justice Bill propose that a conviction should be recorded as a preliminary to dismissal, binding over, or a probation order; and urges H.M. Government to amend the Clauses so that practice which has been followed successfully for thirty years under the Probation of Offenders Act, 1907, may be preserved.

Considerable controversy delayed the progress of the Bill, and the outbreak of war (3 September 1939) caused it to be dropped. A revised Criminal Justice Bill did not become law until 1948, and it did not restore the arrangements set out in the 1907 Act.

From time to time during the 1930s Madeleine is likely to have found herself in contact with her former lover, Jimmy Mallon, but it is not clear how she felt about him at this stage. Seeing him, even in a professional context, may still have been painful to her. He too was a JP, sitting at Toynbee Hall Juvenile Court, and on one occasion he was put on the defensive by an action of hers. This was when, at the 163rd meeting of the executive committee of the Howard League on 24 April 1936, she "reported a case of boys of 15 and 16 years old sentenced by the Toynbee Hall Court to a month's imprisonment on their first charge". Clearly she thought this unacceptable. Jimmy Mallon's reply, reported to the executive committee at its 165th meeting on 26 June 1936, probably struck her as rather lame. It was that, while he was "in principle strongly opposed to the imprisonment of juveniles", he regretted "the exceptional circumstances of the case of the three boys when he had seen no alternative to concurring with the sentence ... passed by the stipendiary".[106]

I have little information about Madeleine's leisure activities and travels in the 1930s, but she was a sociable person with many friends. Mary Hamilton describes how, after a stay in Salzburg in 1936, she joined Madeleine and Grace Usher for a drive back to England, across southern Germany and northern France, in Madeleine's car, remarking:

> Our direction was determined by two wishes: it was characteristic of Madeline [sic] that neither of them were hers, though she was our driver and parent of the whole jaunt.[107]

She goes on to say that Madeleine knew France well, and it is highly likely that the trip just described was one of several or many she made across the English Channel. She had a good knowledge of French too, and is reputed to have found subtitles an irritating distraction when she went to the cinema to see a film in French.

During the war she continued to serve the cause of juvenile justice in London, taking over as Chairman of Stamford House Juvenile Court in 1941. She served also as a trade union representative on the National Arbitration Tribunal. Her nomination by the General Council of the Trades

---

106 Howard League for Penal Reform Archive, Minute Book January 1933–December 1937 (16B/1/2).
107 Hamilton, *Remembering*, p. 207. Both Mary and Grace wanted to visit particular places in Vosges.

Union Congress was announced on 24 July 1940.[108] In the national emergency, compulsory arbitration was imposed to prevent strikes and lock-outs, which were made illegal, and the Tribunal's job was to settle the disputes referred to it. In July 1943 she accepted another important appointment, as a member of the Catering Wages Commission, chaired by Hartley Shawcross, KC. The Commission had a much wider remit than the name suggests, being concerned not only with the wages, conditions of employment, health, and welfare of employees, but also with the whole development of the catering industry to meet the requirements of the public and tourists, including with the way the industry could best be rehabilitated after the war.

Madeleine retained her South Kensington home until the year before she died, but for most of the Second World War did not occupy it.[109] Not later than 1940 she acquired a spacious one-and-a-half-storey seventeenth-century thatched house called Pinders in the "picture-postcard" North Cotswold village of Broad Campden, close to Chipping Campden. Dicky had entered Shrewsbury School as a boarder in September 1938 at the age of thirteen.[110] Teresa (Figure 7), who in London had been a pupil first at Glendower, a preparatory school for girls in Cromwell Road, Kensington, then at St Paul's

---

108 *The Times*, 25 July 1940, p. 2. She is shown as a member of the National Union of General and Municipal Workers, formed in 1924 by the amalgamation of the National Union of General Workers with two other unions.

109 Letter from Madeleine to Dicky Symons, 28 February 1945. Private collection.

110 Madeleine's choice of Shrewsbury may have been influenced by Jean Smith, two of whose brothers had been educated there.

Girls' School, Hammersmith, was admitted to the historic Chipping Campden Grammar School in August 1940. When Madeleine needed to be in London, she was able to take a train from nearby Moreton-in-Marsh to Paddington Station. Pinders and the surrounding area were a safe, healthy, and delightful location for both children and for the reception of other family and friends, including Nancy, who, long considered one of the family, married Ivo Henry Bargrave Deane, a naval officer, on 28 October 1939.

A year later Madeleine herself got married. On 6 December 1939 her Newnham friend Marjorie Eva Robinson, *née* Powell, died after a distressing illness[111] at the age of forty-six, leaving her husband of nineteen years, Harold Roper Robinson, known as Robin, and two children – Anne Elizabeth and Andrew Thomas Roper, aged seventeen and fifteen respectively. The marriage had been a happy one, and the loss of his wife hit Robin hard. Madeleine's friendship with Marjorie had been a long and close one, and she had enjoyed a mutually affectionate relationship with the children and no doubt with Robin as well. Naturally she will have given the three bereaved all the sympathy and support she could, and in this situation she and Robin fell in love with one another. On 25 October 1940 they got married quietly in the Register Office in Moreton-in-Marsh. He was fifty, she forty-five.

---

111 Her death certificate gives her causes of death as myocardial degeneration (disease of the heart muscle), peritonitis, and retroperitonal sarcoma. It and Andrade give her second forename as Eve rather than Eva, which is the name on her birth certificate and in her Newnham College records.

Robin was born on 26 November 1889 in Ulverston, Lancashire, where his father was a solicitor's clerk.[112] From the local secondary school he went on to the University of Manchester, where he studied physics alongside James Chadwick, the discoverer of the neutron, under Ernest Rutherford. So good was his work that, when he was still an undergraduate, he was invited by Rutherford to collaborate with him in a research project. After graduation, he remained in Manchester until 1921 as a lecturer and researcher, with a break of several years during the First World War, when he was an officer in the Royal Artillery and saw service in France and the Near East (1915–1919). In 1921, the year after his marriage to Marjorie, he followed Rutherford to Cambridge. Two years later he moved to Edinburgh, in 1926 to the chair of physics at Cardiff, and in 1930 to the corresponding position at Queen Mary College (QMC),[113] University of London. In 1929 he was elected a Fellow of the Royal Society in recognition of his work on the effect of homogeneous X-rays in liberating electrons. This work was important for the understanding of atomic structure, but it involved a rather narrow field, outside which he never ventured.

At QMC Robin devoted himself not only to the development of his department, but also to the administration of the college and the university. He took his full share of teaching, including courses on the history of science, a subject in which he had long taken an interest. He contin-

112 On Robin's life and career, see especially Andrade.
113 East London College until December 1934.

ued his research through the 1930s, but his last significant scientific paper was published in 1940, which is a clear indication of how his interests and energies were by now concentrated on teaching and administration and also on matters outside the college and university. He was a cultured man, who loved classical French literature as well as English. Among his interests were drama and ballet, and in 1937 he was appointed to represent the University of London on the Boards of The Old Vic and Sadler's Wells. His close involvement with both theatres continued after the Second World War: he was reappointed to the Board of The Old Vic in 1949 and to that of Sadler's Wells in 1951. He was a discriminating collector of old books, especially ones on scientific subjects, and a connoisseur of wine, especially burgundy. Love of France and French productions, whether literary or vinous, was one of the things that he had in common with Madeleine.

During the war QMC's staff and students moved to Cambridge, where they were guests of King's College. It was very soon after the Robinsons arrived in Cambridge that Marjorie died. At the time of Robin's marriage to Madeleine and for more than a year after it his address was 3 West Road – very convenient for King's, the Cavendish Laboratory, and the University Library. Later in the war he and Madeleine occupied a flat in a house called Drumwalt on Long Road, on the southern outskirts of the city and within comfortable reach of the railway station.

At least six feet and three inches tall, Robin was an imposing presence (Figure 9). As a young man, he enjoyed boxing and swimming. As a teacher, colleague, and administrator, he was much liked and respected for his courteousness and generosity, for his energy and enthusiasm, for his clearsightedness in tackling problems, and not least for his sense of humour and humanity – all qualities possessed in abundance by Madeleine as well. It is little wonder that they were attracted to one another.

What Madeleine thought of one of Robin's habits is not, so far as I know, recorded. When he was a young man, he became a heavy pipe-smoker, and remained one until ill health compelled him to restrict his smoking in the last year or two of his life. Of course smoking a pipe was common in those days, but Robin had a penchant for particularly strong, rough, and evil-smelling sorts of tobacco.[114]

Madeleine's marriage no doubt brought her much happiness, although the wartime situation brought obvious difficulties, including the juggling of domestic responsibilities and arrangements with her professional commitments in London. Those responsibilities included not only her own children, but also her stepchildren. At the time of their mother's death Anne and Andrew were at boarding school – Anne at Hawnes School near Ampthill in Bedfordshire, Andrew at Dauntsey's School in Wiltshire. Anne went on to the London School of Economics (LSE), where she took the two-year course for the Social Science Certificate (1941–1943). Like QMC, the LSE had been evacuated to Cambridge. It was accommodated in Peterhouse. Later Anne trained as

---

114   Andrade, p. 163.

a hospital almoner and went on to have a long and successful career in nursing. After leaving Dauntsey's, Andrew joined the Royal Artillery and in the second half of the Second World War served in India, achieving the rank of Major. After the war he read law at King's College, Cambridge, and went on to practise as a solicitor. He was much less close to his father than to his mother's bachelor brother, (John) Dare Powell (1891–1983), who farmed in Shropshire.

During the war Madeleine was usually based in Cambridge in term-time and in Broad Campden during the vacations. While in Cambridge, she will have been in close touch with Newnham College, of which she had been an Associate since 1935. The Associates were and are a group of alumnae who further the interests of the College as a place of education, learning, and research. Madeleine was an Associate until 1951 and again from 1954 to 1957. She was also a member of the College's Governing Body from 1950 to 1952.

Late in the war her happiness was suddenly shattered. Dicky had left Shrewsbury School, aged eighteen, in July 1943 after five fulfilling years. His academic performance, although not outstanding, was satisfactory and solid: in his last year he was in the Classical Lower Sixth form. In his last two terms he was a house monitor (prefect). What he excelled at was sport: as well as playing cricket and soccer quite well, he was in the school's cross-country running VIII and Eton Fives IV. His house was Rigg's Hall, situated on the right of the main entrance-gates to the school (the Moss Gates), a stone's throw from the bronze statue of the soldier, statesman, and poet Sir Philip Sidney (1554–1586), an early

Salopian. On 18 June 1943, towards the end of his last term, he was interviewed in London for the Coldstream Guards. He had served for three years in the school's Junior Training Corps and attained the rank of Lance Corporal. He was also a member of the Home Guard (School Unit). Having passed both parts of "Certificate A", he was on course to become an officer, subject to his obtaining satisfactory reports on his Preliminary Training. He started that training on 30 July 1943. On 24 March 1944 he was gazetted to an emergency commission as a Second Lieutenant (Figure 8). On the same date he started a two-month Street Fighting Wing course given by the London District School of Tactics. Six months later (24 September 1944) he was promoted to the rank of Lieutenant.

At the time of his promotion he was probably serving in the Netherlands, where the Coldstream Guards' Fifth Battalion was involved in "Operation Market Garden" (17–25 September 1944), in which Allied Forces tried but failed to force their way into Germany and across the Rhine. He was certainly serving there in February 1945 as a platoon commander in the Fifth Battalion's Number Two Company. This time the battalion was involved in "Operation Veritable" – an Allied operation to drive the Germans out of the areas they occupied west of the Rivers Maas and Rhine in preparation for crossing the Rhine itself. The operation began on 8 February and finished on 11 March.

On 3 March 1945, only two months before the end of the war in Europe, Madeleine received news which she always hoped she would be spared. It came in a telegram from the War Office, informing her that Dicky "was reported missing believed killed on 21st February 1945".[115] Although the uncertainty about his fate initially allowed a glimmer of hope that he was still alive, it added to her distress. In a letter of 5 March 1945 to the regimental lieutenant-colonel, M.F. Trew, she asked him to pass on any information he might receive, adding:

> I shall be grateful – If possible, I would rather know what happened to him, than just wonder.[116]

It emerged that his platoon was out on a preliminary reconnaisance patrol in the evening of 20 February, when at 21.00 it was ambushed at a frontier post near Gennep. The enemy opened fire at close range from a house on the left of the road. Dicky and another member of the platoon fell. Surviving members took cover and, when the Germans removed Dicky's body, he was seen to be "not moving", unlike the other man, who was captured wounded.[117] It is not clear if his body was ever recovered for burial, but he has a numbered grave (reference II.D.14) in the war cemetery at Mook in the province of Limburg. The gravestone gives his date of death as 20 February 1945, not, as Madeleine was earlier given to understand, 21 February. Gennep is only about twenty miles, as the crow flies, from Arnhem, where

---

115 Private collection.
116 Coldstream Guards Archives.
117 According to Michael Howard and John Sparrow, *The Coldstream Guards, 1920–1946*, p. 354, the incident claimed the lives of two guardsmen as well as the life of Dicky.

on 17 October 1586 Sir Philip Sidney died from wounds he sustained fighting the Spanish at Zutphen. Given that Dicky spent five years of his tragically short life within sight of Sidney's statue at Shrewsbury School, the proximity of the place where he died to the place where Sidney met his end strikes one as rather eerie.

A parent's life can never be the same again after the premature loss of a beloved child, but, as in earlier times of unhappiness, Madeleine found the courage and determination to carry on with life and work. This time at least she had a loving husband, as well as close friends, to comfort and support her, and of course she in turn needed to support Teresa, now aged eighteen. Dicky's death was a severe loss for her too. The depth and duration of Madeleine's feelings of loss can be gauged from the way they surfaced at the wedding of Dicky's cousin Douglas Boyd on 27 February 1954. She was fond of Douglas and happy for him, but the event took place just a week after the ninth anniversary of Dicky's death, and the thoughts of him and what might have been had her in tears.

By the end of the academic year 1944–1945 the war was over, and there was to be no return to the flat in Cambridge. Queen Mary College returned to London for the start of the new academic year in the autumn of 1945, and, except in vacations and sometimes at weekends, the Robinsons were living in Madeleine's Kensington home at 18 Pelham Crescent, where in 1946 they acquired an interesting new neighbour, the ballerina Margot Fonteyn, who resided at number 19 when she was not in her flat in Covent Garden.

Given Robin's close involvement with The Old Vic and Sadler's Wells, one wonders whether it was just a matter of chance that Fonteyn came to live next door. Certainly the two would have had plenty to talk about whenever their busy lives allowed any opportunity for conversation.

At QMC Robin wrestled with the problems of damaged buildings and a shortage of staff. He continued to teach, but never returned to serious research work. Instead he devoted his time and energy to administration both in the college and in the university. He was vice-principal of QMC from 1946 to 1953 and at the same time served on many university committees. Health problems prompted him to retire both as vice-principal and as professor of physics in 1953, but in 1954 he was persuaded to accept appointment first as deputy vice-chancellor, then, three months later, as vice-chancellor of the university – a post he held until October 1955, when poor health forced his resignation. He suffered from diabetes mellitus, and his heart was not strong.

Madeleine was fully supportive of Robin with respect to his administrative duties, accompanying him to many of the social functions which his positions involved and entertaining colleagues and friends of his at home. She was also supportive of his interests in ballet and theatre. But the time she gave to him did not prevent her from continuing with her own work as a juvenile magistrate and as one deeply committed to the interests of the delinquent young and to the provision of the security and care she insisted they needed. At Christmas 1946 she was one of eight women who signed a letter appealing for donations to save St Clare's Hostel for

Girls in Hampstead.[118] She took a close interest in the work and report of the Care of Children Committee, chaired by Dame Myra Curtis. The Howard League gave evidence to the Committee, whose report was presented to the House of Commons in 1946. The following year she published an article, applauding the emphasis placed on the individual needs of the child, but highly critical of some of the report's proposals and omissions.[119] The report led to the passing of the Children Act 1948. During the passage of the Children Bill through Parliament she expressed surprise, in her capacity as chairman of Stamford House Juvenile Court, "that the legal rights of parents and guardians under the Bill have received little public attention".[120]

As when she was a trade union officer, so in her work as a magistrate, she interested herself in situations and developments abroad as well as at home. In the autumn of 1948 she and Margery Fry represented the Howard League at a meeting, held in Paris, of non-governmental bodies concerned with penal questions.[121] The meeting took place in the Palais de Chaillot under the auspices of the United Nations. On 10 December 1948 the same venue saw the adoption by the UN General Assembly of the Universal Declaration of Human Rights.

---

118 *The Times*, 24 December 1946, p. 5.
119 Madeleine J. Robinson, "Child Care: The Curtis Report", *The Howard Journal of Criminal Justice* 7, 2 (July 1947), pp. 117–120.
120 *The Times*, 19 May 1948, p. 5.
121 Howard League Archive, Minute Book November 1947–June 1951 (16/B/1/5), 274th meeting of the executive committee, 19 November 1948.

In the 1950s Madeleine continued to be very active on various fronts – as a juvenile magistrate, in the Magistrates' Association, in the Howard League, and as a member of Home Office committees and deputations. Her main concern continued to be the importance of education and reform rather than punishment, and of having the right sorts of people and institutions to provide successful outcomes. Space allows mention of just a few examples of her representations and interventions.

In a letter of 19 February 1950 to Lord Templewood,[122] chairman of the Council of the Magistrates' Association and president of the Howard League, she was critical of the failure of the Home Office to collect reliable statistics about the success or otherwise of the treatment of children who have appeared before juvenile courts and been sent to Approved Schools or placed on probation. She complained too about the frequent lack of a proper follow-up of such cases (for example of older adolescent girls, most of whom "are budding prostitutes rather than offenders"), and stressed the need for objective research to be undertaken by professionally qualified investigators, and for the funds for this work to be provided.

Madeleine was one of those appointed by the Minister of Education on 4 October 1950 "to enquire into and report upon the medical, educational and social problems relating to maladjusted children, with reference to their treatment within the educational system". The report of the Committee,

---

122 Templewood Papers.

chaired by Dr. J.E.A. Underwood, was published in 1955.

After the Franklin Committee produced its review of punishments in prisons, Borstal institutions, Approved Schools, and Remand Homes in 1951, Madeleine published a critical review of its report on punishments in Approved Schools and Remand Homes.[123] She applauded the Committee for following the Curtis Committee in stressing the individual needs of children and recommending "better provision for the backward and the maladjusted, for psychiatric observation and for improvements in training and working conditions designed to secure the right kind of staff", but criticised it for giving unhelpful statistics and above all for its "uncritical acceptance of the present situation as regards punishments". At this time caning and deprivation of liberty and food were not uncommon in children's homes. Her own view was that such punishments, so far from being efficacious, only created more problems.

Another report that appeared in 1951 and was reviewed by Madeleine the following year was the Sixth Report on the Work of the Children's Committee[124] – the first report of the Committee since January 1938, the long delay being mainly due to the war. She praised parts of the report, including its "objective statement of the nature of juvenile delinquency and of the war-time and post-war developments" and its focus on the psychiatric treatment of delinquents,

---

123 Madeleine J. Robinson, J.P., *British Journal of Delinquency* 2, 4 (April 1952), pp. 320–321.
124 Madeleine Robinson, *The Howard Journal of Criminal Justice* 8, 3 (July 1952), pp. 186–188.

but was critical of its silence on the important subjects of adoption and probation. She was critical too of the age of criminal responsibility in the United Kingdom being, as it was at that time, as low as eight, and one can safely assume that she would not have been favourably impressed if she had been told that in 2017 the age of criminal responsibility in England, Wales, and Northern Ireland would be ten, while in Scotland it would still be eight.

By no means all of Madeleine's fellow-magistrates thought the same way as she did about the best way to handle young offenders. A few days after the Annual Meeting of the Magistrates' Association held in New Hall, Lincoln's Inn, on 16 October 1952, she wrote to Margery Fry. She warmly congratulated her on the lecture she had given on "Whither Justice?", adding that many in her audience wanted her to broadcast a similar talk. She continued:

> On the other hand I feel this was about the toughest annual meeting we have ever had and I suspect that they had come up to down us on Corporal Punishment. Sometimes I wonder whether we are making any headway in educating magistrates – I have an old friend who has got a job with UNECO[125] to develop visual aids to education in Jugoslavia; I feel he might be better occupied here as I am sure many of our members are illiterate![126]

---

125 United Nations Educational and Cultural Organization. UNECO had actually become UNESCO in November 1945, when "Scientific" was added to its name.
126 Letter of 22 October 1952, Somerville College, Oxford, Archives, Margery Fry Papers, Box 26.

At this time both Madeleine and Margery were members of a Howard League sub-committee on training schemes for new magistrates. Madeleine was also chairman of the Visiting Justices at Holloway Prison.

Madeleine will have been disappointed, but probably not surprised when, on 12 February 1953, the announcement of the result of a referendum held by the Magistrates' Association revealed that its members had voted by more than two to one in favour of courts having power to order corporal punishment for crimes of violence. At the same time it was reported that members of the National Association of Probation Officers had declared themselves opposed to the reintroduction of corporal punishment by a majority of six to one.[127] Such punishment had been prohibited under the Criminal Justice Act 1948.

Madeleine was a member of the Departmental Committee on the Adoption of Children, chaired by Sir Gerald Hurst. The unanimously agreed "Hurst Report" was published in September 1954, but, to the disappointment and alarm of its members[128] and no doubt many thousands of other people interested in the welfare of children, Parliament took no early action to implement its recommendations. Eventually the report led to the Adoption Act 1958, which came into force on 1 April 1959. Sadly, Madeleine was not to see that day; nor indeed was the Committee's chairman, who died on 27 October 1957.

127 "Birch for Crimes of Violence: Magistrates' Vote", *The Times*, 13 February 1953, p. 6.
128 Letter to *The Times*, 30 January 1956, p. 7.

On 28 November 1955, just a month after Madeleine's husband, Robin, retired from the vice-chancellorship of the University of London, he died in a chair at home after suffering a coronary thrombosis, with diabetes given as the second cause of death. He had celebrated his sixty-sixth birthday two days earlier. Although his death was sudden, it may not have been wholly unexpected, given that his health had been poor for some time, but it was undoubtedly a heavy blow for Madeleine, after fifteeen years of marriage, to lose the companionship and support of the husband to whom she was devoted.

A few weeks after Robin's death Madeleine made a new will (10 February 1956). In it she named Teresa as sole beneficiary, while stipulating that, if she "shall predecease me leaving a child or children living at my death", such child or children shall inherit her estate on reaching the age of twenty-one, and adding, tellingly:

> I declare that in this clause the phrase "child or children" shall be deemed to include any natural child whether legitimate or illegitimate and any adopted child.

Teresa left Chipping Campden Grammar School in 1942. Later she did a variety of work, but details of the order, timing, and precise nature of it are lacking. She spent time at the United Nations in Geneva and New York and with *The Spectator* in London. At *The Spectator* she met the distinguished journalist and writer T.E. ("Peter") Utley, its associate editor from 1954 to 1955. He was to be godfather to her daughter born in 1960. On 3 November 1958 she married (Gerald Maurice) Stephen ("Stevie") Corbett, a divorcee ten years her senior, at Fulham Register Office. The couple had two children – Emma Teresa (born 2 June 1960) and (James) Justin (born 12 October 1961). Teresa died suddenly in Westminster Hospital on 2 May 1972. The cause of death was a dissecting aortic aneurysm caused by high blood pressure – a rare condition, particularly for someone of her age. She was only forty-five. Stevie, who from the early 1960s worked for the National Trust, died on 1 October 1992.

Madeleine did not live to see Teresa married. A few months after Robin's death she left 18 Pelham Crescent, her main home for twenty-nine years, and moved the very short distance – almost literally just round the corner – to Flat 2, 55 Onslow Square. It is not entirely clear what prompted the move. Probably the main consideration was a wish to downsize, although her new abode was still quite grand and spacious. Sadly, she was not to have the enjoyment of it for long before her health deteriorated sharply. One of the last social engagements she fulfilled was a party given on 15 November 1956 by her friend of over forty years Jean Smith in the latter's flat at 6 Ashley Court, Morpeth Terrace, close by Westminster Cathedral. The guest-list is preserved among the papers of Jean's youngest brother, Henry, for whom she wrote it.[129] He kept it because Jean added brief biographical notes on several of those invited.

---

129 Private collection (MFS).

Significantly, there is no such note on Madeleine, whom Henry had known since he was a teenager and stayed with the Symons family at Hadley Lodge.

Four months after Jean's party, on Thursday, 21 March 1957, Madeleine died at home of acute myocarditis and measles. She was sixty-one. In the days that followed, exceptionally warm tributes were paid to her by some of those with whom she had been in close personal and/or professional contact over the years. They included the well-informed writer of the anonymous obituary printed in *The Times* the day after her death[130] and the authors of three further notices that appeared in the same newspaper in the following days – James Eugene McColl, MP,[131] "a group of friends",[132] and Lady Cynthia Colville.[133] James McColl, appointed a JP in 1938, had been chairman of North London Juvenile Court since 1949. Lady Cynthia was made a JP in 1929 and, after gaining experience in the East London Juvenile Court at Toynbee Hall, became a juvenile court chairman. Another link she had with Madeleine was that for thirty years she was a Woman of the Bedchamber to Queen Mary, patroness of the Mary Macarthur Home(s). That was from 1923 until the Queen's death in 1953. The tributes make moving reading, presenting a vivid picture of a woman who was not only much respected for her wisdom, energy, and clarity of thought and speech, but also

---

130 *The Times*, 22 March 1957, p. 10.
131 *The Times*, 26 March 1957, p. 13. The writer only gives his initials, J.E.McC.
132 *The Times*, 29 March 1957, p. 13.
133 *The Times*, 3 April 1957, p. 13.

much loved for her kindness, modesty, sense of humour, and charm.

On 12 April 1957 a memorial service was held for Madeleine at the Church of St Bartholomew the Great in the City of London. Among those present, in addition to members of her family, were close friends of long standing, including Dorothy Garrod[134] and Jean Smith, representatives of the Home Secretary and Lord Privy Seal, the Ministry of Labour, the Children's Department of the Home Office, and the numerous institutions and organisations with which she had been associated.[135] These included the Visiting Committee of Holloway Prison, the Holloway Discharged Prisoners' Aid Society, the Magistrates' Association, the Family Planning Association, the Society of Juvenile Probation Officers, Metropolitan Women's Police, and the Industrial Welfare Society.

---

134 Dorothy, as well as paying tribute to a friend she had had since they were pupils at Birklands School, was representing Past Associates of Newnham College. Present Associates of the college were also represented, and at the annual meeting of the Associates on 27 June 1957 all present stood in tribute to Madeleine, and a eulogistic resolution was read and passed.
135 *The Times*, 13 April 1957, p. 8; 15 April 1957, p. 12.

References

Abbott, Clare. *Faithful of Days: The Story of Robert Crighton, Master Mariner.* Oxford and Shrewsbury: YouCaxton Publications, 2014.

Andrade, E.N. da C. "Harold Roper Robinson 1889–1955". *Biographical Memoirs of Fellows of the Royal Society* 3 (1957), pp. 160–172.

Birklands School Magazine, Christmas Term 1913–Christmas Term 1923. Imperial War Museum Library, Lambeth, catalogue reference E.J.1106.

Bondfield, Margaret. *A Life's Work.* London: Hutchinson, [1949].

Graves, Pamela M. *Labour Women: Women in British Working-Class Politics 1918–1939.* Cambridge: Cambridge University Press, 1994.

Hamilton, Mary Agnes. *Mary Macarthur: A Biographical Sketch.* London: Leonard Parsons, 1925.

―――. *Remembering My Good Friends.* London: Jonathan Cape, 1944.

Horan, Alice. "Madeleine Symons: A Tribute". *The Labour Woman* 45, 5 (May 1957), pp. 71, 78.

Howard League for Penal Reform Archive. Modern Records Centre, University of Warwick Library, Coventry.

Howard, Michael, and John Sparrow. *The Coldstream Guards, 1920–1946.* London: Oxford University Press, 1957.

Hunt, Cathy. *The National Federation of Women Workers, 1906–1921.*

Basingstoke and New York: Palgrave Macmillan, 2014.

Law, Cheryl. *Women: A Modern Political Dictionary*. London and New York: I.B. Tauris, 2000.

Logan, Anne. *Feminism and Criminal Justice: A Historical Perspective*. Basingstoke and New York: Palgrave Macmillan, 2008.

―――. "Feminist Criminology in Britain circa 1920–1960: Education, Agency, and Activism Outside the Academy". In *Women, Education, and Agency, 1600–2000*, edited by Jean Spence, Sarah Jane Aiston, Maureen M. Meikle. New York and London: Routledge, 2010, pp. 204–222.

Macaulay, Rose. *Potterism: A Tragi-farcical Tract*. London: W. Collins, 1920.

Mary Macarthur Holiday Trust Archive. London Metropolitan University Archives and Special Collections, Holloway Road Library, London.

Newnham College *Roll Letter 1916*. Cambridge: Newnham College, 1916.

Post-Office Greenock Directory for 1863–1864. Greenock: Joseph Blair, 1863.

Report of the Departmental Committee on the Social Services in Courts of Summary Jurisdiction. Presented by the Secretary of State for the Home Department to Parliament by Command of His Majesty. London: His Majesty's Stationery Office, 1936.

Report of the Royal Commission on Lunacy and Mental Disorder. Presented to Parliament by Command of His Majesty. London: His Majesty's Stationery Office, 1926.

Smith, Jean Isabel. *Interdepartmental*. Manuscript notebook recording incidents and conversations witnessed by the writer, mainly in 1916–1917. Private collection (MFS).

Smith, Martin Ferguson. *Dearest Jean: Rose Macaulay's Letters to a Cousin*. Manchester: Manchester University Press, 2011; paperback edition with revisions, Manchester University Press, 2017.

S[ymons], M[adeleine] J[ane]. Report on a General Meeting of

Newnham College Society for Women's Suffrage. *Thersites* no. 46 (9 December 1915): no page numbers.

Templewood Papers. Part XVI: *Penal Reform*: File 6: *Treatment of Juvenile Offenders*. Letter from Madeleine J. Robinson, 19 February 1950. Cambridge University Library.

TUC Library Collections, London Metropolitan University.

Whitman, Walt. "Song of Myself", first published untitled in *Leaves of Grass*. Brooklyn, New York: Self-published, 1855.

Whittier, John Greenleaf. "The Three Bells". In *The Poetical Works of John Greenleaf Whittier*, new edition. London: Macmillan, 1893, pp. 463–464.

Index

Note: "n" after a page reference indicates a footnote on that page, "nn" more than one footnote. Numbers in **bold** are not of pages, but of the illustrations on pp. 56–60.

Abbott, Clare 17, 48n, 67
   Faithful of Days 17n, 68n
Adelphi, The (London) 54
Adoption Act (1958) 95
adoption of children 67, 94, 95, 96
   by Madeleine Symons 67
Adoption of Children,
   Departmental Committee on
   the (Hurst Report, 1954) 95
Adoption of Children Act (1926) 67
Anderson, Anne ("Nancy")
   Elizabeth **3**, 40, 42, 67, 82
Anderson, James 42
Anderson, Mary Reid *see*
   Macarthur, Mary Reid
Anderson, William ("Will")
   Crawford 40–41
Antarctic (ship) 16
Antwerp 16, 17–18, 19

British consulate-general 18, 19n
Approved Schools 92, 93
Arbitration, Court of 38, 39
Arnhem, Netherlands 88
Arnot, Robert ("Robin") Page 52–53
Australia 18

Barcelona 26, 27, 31
Barker, Grace *see* Usher, Grace
Barnet 20, 30, 31
Basevi, George 68
BBC 77
Bedales School 42
Belgrave Square, London 68
Bilbao 26
Birkenhead 16
Birklands/New Birklands School 21–22, 24, 34n, 36, 44, 99n

103

Birklands School Magazine 21–22, 34n, 35, 36, 48nn
Bombay 49
Bondfield, Margaret Grace 28n, 35, 40n, 43, 46
   A Life's Work 40n
Borstal 93
Bow Street Police Court 52
Boyd, Douglas Gordon 89
Brighton 47
British Communist Party (BCP) 52
British Medical Association (BMA) 77–78
Broad Campden 81, 86
Brooke, Dorothy, *née* Lamb 45
Brooke, John Reeve 45
Buckingham Street (no. 14), London 49, 68

Camberwell 15, 19
Cambridge 23, 24, 25, 26, 83, 84, 85, 86, 89
   see also Cavendish Laboratory; Fitzwilliam Museum; Girton College; Great Shelford; King's College; Newnham College; Peterhouse
Card, Mrs 27n
Cardiff, University College of South Wales and Monmouthshire 83
Care of Children Committee (Curtis Report, 1946) 91, 93
Catering Wages Commission (1943–1945) 81
Cave, George, Viscount 47
Cave Committee of Inquiry (1921–1922) 47
Cavendish Laboratory, Cambridge 84
Caxton Hall, London 35, 78
   Juvenile Court 71
Central Criminal Court (Old Bailey) 53
Ceylon 48, 49
Chadwick, James 83
Chegwyn, Elizabeth Helen, *née* Cox 21
Child Guidance Inter-Clinic Conference (1939) 77
children, adoption of *see* adoption of children
   treatment of offenders 71–72, 77–78, 79–80, 90–95 *see also* Care of Children Committee; juvenile courts
Children Act (1948) 91
Children and Young Persons Act (1933) 72
Children's Committee, Sixth Report on the Work of (1951) 93
Chipping Campden 81
   Grammar School 82, 96
Clough, Blanche Athena ("B.A.") 24
Clyde, River 15
Coldstream Guards 87–88
Collins, Beatrice Nellie 55n
Colville, Lady (Helen) Cynthia, *née* Milnes 98
Conservative Party 55
Corbett, Emma Teresa 42n, 68, 97
Corbett, (Gerald Maurice) Stephen 97
Corbett, (James) Justin 97

Corbett, Teresa Mary *see* Symons, Teresa Mary
corporal punishment 93, 94, 95
Cotswolds 81
Covent Garden 89
Crewe, Lady Peggy (Crewe-Milnes, Margaret Etienne Hannah, *née* Primrose) 70n
Crighton, Alexander Thomson 18, 22–23
Crighton, Alfred James 18
Crighton, Jane ("Jeannie"), *née* McKeich 15n
Crighton, Jane, *née* Thomson 15, 17, 20, 23
Crighton, Mary Catharine *see* Symons, Mary Catharine
Crighton, Mary Elizabeth, *née* Chapman 17
Crighton, Robert (1821–1882) 16–17
Crighton, Robert (1854–1924) 17, 18, 19, 49
Crighton, William Bell 18
Criminal Justice Act (1948) 79, 95
Criminal Justice Bill (1939) 78–79
criminal responsibility, age of 94
Curtis, Myra 91
    see also Care of Children Committee

Daily News, The 53–55, 65
Dauntsey's School 85, 86
Deane, Anne Elizabeth *see* Anderson, Anne ("Nancy") Elizabeth
Deane, Ivo Henry Bargrave 82
Deane, James 42n
De Crespigny Park (no. 9), London 15
Delaunay Belleville motor car 20, 32
Denmark Hill, London 15, 19
Departmental Committee on the Adoption of Children *see* Adoption of Children, Departmental Committee on the
Departmental Committee on the Social Services in Courts of Summary Jurisdiction (1934–1936) 73–75, 76, 78
Dilke House, Malet Street, London 27
Donaldson Line 18

East London College *see* Queen Mary College
East London Juvenile Court 98
Edinburgh University 83
Education, Minister of 92

Fairacres, Oxford 66n
Family Planning Association 99
First World War 22, 23, 26, 35, 38, 45, 83
Fitzwilliam Museum, Cambridge 68
Fonteyn, Margot 89–90
France 19, 80, 83, 84
Franklin Committee Report (1951) 93
Fry, Julian Edward 42
Fry, Roger Eliot 42
Fry, (Sara) Margery 42–43, 91, 94–95
Fulham Register Office 97
Fulham Road, London 68

Gables, The, Ongar 43, 69
Gardiner, Alfred George 65
Gardiner, Stella Katherine *see*
    Mallon, Stella Katherine
Garrod, Dorothy Annie Elizabeth
    21–22, 23, 23n, 29, 30nn, 99
Garvin, Viola, *née* Taylor 46n
Geneva 41, 64n, 96
Gennep, Netherlands 88
George V, King 43
Germany 80, 87
Gibraltar 48
Girton College, Cambridge 25
Glasgow 16
Glendower School, Kensington 81
Godolphin School, Salisbury 26
Great Shelford, near Cambridge 26
Greenock 15, 48, 53

Hadley Lodge, near Barnet 20, 21,
    23, 28–33, 42, 98
    sale of 32, 42
Hamilton, Mary ("Molly") Agnes,
    née Adamson 19, 40n, 45, 80
    Mary Macarthur 40n
    Remembering My Good
    Friends 19n, 45nn, 80n
Hammersmith 54, 82
Hargrave House, Stansted 69
Harland & Wolff 18, 49
Hatfield Polytechnic 22n
Hawaii 48
Hawnes School, near Ampthill 85
Henley, Mary 49n
High Court of Justice, Chancery
    Division 67
Highgate, London 21
Holloway Discharged Prisoners
    Aid Society 99
Holloway Prison, Visiting Justices
    at 95, 99
Home Guard 29n, 87
Home Office 52, 72n, 74, 77, 92
    Children's Department 99
Home Secretary 51, 73, 75, 99
    see also Joynson-Hicks,
    William
Hong Kong 49
Honolulu 48, 49
House of Commons 91
House of Representatives 17n
Howard League for Penal Reform
    43, 71, 77, 78, 79, 91, 92,
    95
Hurst, Gerald Berkeley 95
Hurst Report (1954) *see* Adoption
    of Children, Departmental
    Committee on the
Huxley, Aldous Leonard 44

Imperial War Museum, Lambeth 22
Incitement to Mutiny Act (1797)
    52
Independent Labour Party 40
India 43, 86
Industrial Welfare Society 99
International Socialist Conference
    (1920) 41

Jameson, Margaret Ethel
    ("Storm") 45
Japan 48, 49
Jewson, Dorothea ("Dorothy")
    28, 35
Johnson, Andrew (President of the
    United States) 17n

Jones, John ("Jack") Joseph (1873–1941) 40
Joynson-Hicks (originally Hicks), William 51
Justice(s) of the Peace, female 43, 49, 52, 53, 70, 71, 98
Juvenile Court Justices, London Panel of 71
juvenile courts 70, 71, 72–73, 77–80, 92, 98
    Caxton Hall 71
    North London 98
    Stamford House 71, 80, 91
    Toynbee Hall (East London) 79, 98
juvenile offenders *see* children, treatment of offenders

Kensington 44, 68, 81, 89
Kensington Petty Sessions Court 71
Kilby (ship) 16
King's College, Cambridge 84, 86
King's Cross Station, London 28
Knollys House, Bloomsbury 27–28

Labour, Minister of 38
Labour, Ministry of 45, 99
Labour Party 19, 28, 45, 47, 49
    Conferences (1920) 41; (1921) 47; (1922) 47
    Executive Committee 47, 49
    Women's Panel 47
    see also Independent Labour Party
Labour Research Department 52
Labour Women, National Conference of (1920) 41
Lancashire 83

Lawrence, (Arabella) Susan 25, 28n, 35, 41, 43, 47
League of Nations 32
Leighton, Mary Anne 21n
Limburg, Netherlands 88
Littlewood-Clarke, Herbert Dell 49n
Liverpool 16
Logan, Anne Frances Helen 23, 24n, 33n, 62
London, University of 83, 84, 90, 96
    see also Queen Mary College
London District School of Tactics 87
London Fever Hospital 31
London Probation Committee (1937–1940) 75
London School of Economics (LSE) 85
Lord Privy Seal 99

Maas, River 87
Macarthur, Mary Reid 34–44, 45, 46, 64, 65
    death 41
    marriage 40
    see also Mary Macarthur Holiday Home(s)
Macaulay, (Emilie) Rose 26, 32–33, 44–45, 54, 62–67
    Potterism 32–33
    see also Smith, Martin Ferguson, *Dearest Jean*
McColl, James Eugene 98
MacDonald, James Ramsay 45
Maconochie (food manufacturer) 38
Magistrates' Association 71, 72n, 76, 77, 78, 92, 94, 95, 99

Mallon, James ("Jimmy") Joseph
    5, 35, 40, 43, 47, 64–65,
    68, 79
    lover of Madeleine Symons
    and father of Teresa Symons
    64–65, 68, 79
    warden of Toynbee Hall 64
Mallon, Mary Ann, *née* O'Hare
    62n
Mallon, Stella Katherine, *née*
    Gardiner 65
Malwa (ship) 48
Manchester, University of 83
Manila 49
Marlborough College 30
Marsh, T.W.C. 75
Mary, Queen 43–44, 69, 98
    see also Queen Mary's
    Needlework Guild; Queen's
    Work for Women Fund
Mary Macarthur Holiday Home(s)
    for Working Women 43–44,
    61, 68–69, 98
    Committee of Management
    43, 61, 68, 69
    Extension Fund Appeal
    Committee 69
    see also Gables; Hargrave
    House
Mathy, Heinrich 29
matrimonial cases 73, 74, 76
Mecklenburgh Square (no. 34),
    London 27, 64
mental illness and its treatment
    50–51, 77–78, 93
    see also Royal Commission
    on Lunacy and Mental
    Disorder

Mental Treatment Act (1930) 50
Mersey, River 16
Metropolitan Women's Police 99
Monken Hadley 20, 31
Montana sur Randogne,
    Switzerland 31
Mook, Netherlands 88
Moreton-in-Marsh 82
Morpeth Terrace, London 97
Munitions, Ministry of 26, 36, 45
Munitions Court, Metropolitan 35
Munitions of War Act (1915) 36

National Anti-Sweating League
    (NASL) 35
National Arbitration Tribunal
    80–81
National Association of Probation
    Officers 70, 71, 76, 77, 95
National Federation of Women
    Workers (NFWW) 34–36,
    38, 40, 46, 70
National Labour Club 70
National Trust 97
National Union of General (and
    Municipal) Workers 46, 49,
    53, 81n
    Women Workers' Section 46,
    49
National Union of Women's
    Suffrage Societies 25
Netherlands 87–88
New Birklands School *see*
    Birklands/New Birklands
    School
New York 16, 17, 49, 96
Newnham College, Cambridge
    23–25, 26, 48n, 82, 86, 99n

Associates 86, 99n
Governing Body 86
Political Debating Society 23
Sidgwick Hall 23
Society for Women's Suffrage 23–25
Thersites (College magazine) 24, 26
Norfolk 63, 65
   see also Sheringham
North London Juvenile Court 98

Odessa 26
Old Vic, The 84, 90
Olympic (ship) 49
Ongar 43, 44
Onslow Square (no. 55), Kensington 97
"Operation Market Garden" (WW2) 87
"Operation Veritable" (WW2) 87
Oxford 23, 66n, 72, 73

P&O (Pacific & Orient) Company 48
Paddington Station, London 82
Palais de Chaillot, Paris 91
Paris 23, 91
Pelham Crescent, Kensington 68
   (no. 18) 68, 89, 97
   (no. 19) 89
Penal Reform League 71
Peterhouse, Cambridge 85
Petersfield 42, 63
Pinders, Broad Campden 81–82
Potters Bar 29, 30, 33
   Oakmere Park 29
Powell, (John) Dare 86

Powell, Marjorie Eva *see* Robinson, Marjorie Eva
Prentice, Frank Bernard 30
President Taft (ship) 49
Princes Gardens (no. 44), Kensington 44, 45
prison reform 77
   see also Holloway Prison, Visiting Justices at; Howard League for Penal Reform; Penal Reform League
probation 71, 72nn, 73, 74, 75, 76, 78–79, 92, 94
   see also London Probation Committee; National Association of Probation Officers; Society of Juvenile Probation Officers
Probation of Offenders Act (1907) 74, 79

Queen Mary College (QMC), formerly East London College 83, 84, 85, 89–90
Queen Mary's Needlework Guild 43
Queen's Work for Women Fund 43

Red Star Line 17, 18
Remand Homes 93
Rendel, (Frances) Elinor 24
Representation of the People (Equal Franchise) Act (1928) 52
Rhine, River 87
Rigg's Hall, Shrewsbury School 86
Robinson, Andrew Thomas Roper 82, 85–86

Robinson, Anne Elizabeth 82, 85–86
Robinson, Harold Roper ("Robin") **9**, 82–85, 89–90, 96, 97
Robinson, Madeleine Jane *see* Symons, Madeleine Jane
Robinson, Marjorie Eva, *née* Powell 25, 82, 83, 84
Royal Artillery 83, 86
Royal Commission on Lunacy and Mental Disorder (1924–1926) 50–51, 52
Royal Geographical Society 19
Royal Society 83
Royde-Smith, Naomi Gwladys 44–45, 46
Russia 41
Rutherford, Ernest 83

Sadleir, Edith ("Betty"), *née* Tupper-Carey 45
Sadleir (originally Sadler), Michael Thomas Harvey 45
Sadler's Wells Theatre 84, 90
St Albans 21
St Bartholomew the Great's Church, City of London 99
St Clare's Hostel for Girls, Hampstead 90
St Pancras Station, London 23
St Paul's Girls' School, Hammersmith 81–82
Salzburg 80
San Francisco 49
San Francisco (ship) 16, 17n
Saturday Westminster Gazette 44
Sayers, Dorothy Leigh 26

Scarborough 41
Second World War 69, 79, 80–81, 84–89
Shanghai 49
Sharp, Kate 30
Shawcross, Hartley William 81
Sheffield 40
Sheringham 62, 63
Shrewsbury School 30, 81, 86–87, 89
Sidney, Philip 86, 89
Sierre, Switzerland 31
Simpson, Ellen 62
Sinclair, Rebecca Cecilia 55
Singapore 49
Smith, Anne Georgiana, *née* Macaulay 26–27
Smith, Charles Stewart 26, 27n
Smith, Henry Ferguson 30, 97–98
Smith, James ("Jim") Stewart 30–31
Smith, Jean Isabel 26–30, 32, 33, 36–37, 44, 54, 62, 63, 65, 66n, 67, 81n, 97, 98, 99
  "Hadley Lodge Weekend" 28
  Interdepartmental 29, 37
  Shepherd of Souls 66n
Smith, Laura Mary 21
Smith, Martin Ferguson
  Dearest Jean: Rose Macaulay's Letters to a Cousin 33n, 44n, 54n, 62, 63n, 64n, 66n
Social Science Certificate 85
Society for Equal Citizenship 33
Society of Juvenile Probation Officers 99
Southampton 18, 49
Southborough, Baron (Hopwood,

Francis John Stephens) 51
Southborough Committee (1925–1927) 51–52, 61
Spanish flu 40–41
Spectator, The 96
Stamford House Juvenile Court 71, 80, 91
Stansted 69
stillbirths, registration of 40n
Strachey, Rachel ("Ray") Conn, *née* Costelloe 24
Stroh, Bertha 20
suffrage, women's 23–25, 52
   see also National Union of Women's Suffrage Societies; Newnham College, Society for Women's Suffrage; Representation of the People (Equal Franchise) Act; Society for Equal Citizenship
Sweated Industries, Exhibition of 43
Switzerland 31, 41
Symon, Isabella, *née* Todd 15
Symon(s), Charles 15, 16
Symons (born Symon), George Todd **1**, 15–16, 18–20, 31
   birth 15
   death 31
   marriage 18–19
Symons, G.T. & Co. 20
Symons, Madeleine Jane, later Robinson **2, 3, 4, 6, 7, 9**, *passim*
Symons, Mary Catharine, *née* Crighton **2**, 15, 16, 17, 18, 19, 27, 31, 41–42, 62
   birth 16
   death 31, 41–42
   marriage 18–19
Symons, Terence Richard ("Dicky") **8**, 67–68, 81, 86–89
   birth and adoption 67
   death 87–89
   education 81, 86–87
   military service 87–89
Symons, Teresa Mary **6, 7**, 62–68, 81–82, 89, 96–97
   adoption 67
   birth 62, 65
   death 97
   education 81–82, 96
   marriage 97
   paternity 63–64, 68

Tempest, Wulstan Joseph 29n
Templewood, Viscount (Hoare, Samuel John Gurney) 92
Tenyo Maru (ship) 49
Thorne (originally Thorn), William ("Will") James 53–55
Three Bells (ship) 16
Todd, George 15
Toynbee Hall 64, 65
   Juvenile Court 79, 98
Trade Boards 35, 39–40, 47, 64
   Act (1909) 35, 47
Trades Union Congress (TUC)
   General Council 53, 80–81
   Parliamentary Committee 40, 46
   Trade Boards Advisory Council 47
   Women's Group 46
Tranmere 16

Trew, Maurice Frederick 88
Tuckwell, Gertrude Mary 35, 40n, 43, 70, 71

Ulverston 83
Underwood, John Ernest Alfred 93
Underwood Committee (1955) 92–93
UNE(S)CO 94
United Nations 91, 96
    General Assembly 91
United States 18, 48, 49
Universal Declaration of Human Rights (1948) 91
Usher, Grace, *née* Barker 44, 45, 62–64, 67, 80
Usher, Herbert Brough 45, 62–64, 67
Utley, Thomas Edward ("Peter") 96–97

Victoria & Albert Museum 68
Vosges 45, 80n

Wall, J.I., Miss (Home Office, Children's Department) 74
Wandsworth, London 19
War Cabinet Committee on Women in Industry (1918) 38
War Office 88
Webb, (Martha) Beatrice, *née* Potter 70n
Welbeck Street (no. 27), London 62
West Ham Town Council 53
Westley, Jane Reid, *née* Macarthur 42
Westminster Gazette 45
Westminster Hospital 97
Westminster Police Court 75
White Star Line 49

Whitman, Walt 17
    "Song of Myself" 17n
Whittier, John Greenleaf 17
    "The Three Bells" 17n
Willway, (Alfred) Cedric Cowan 75
Wolfe, Humbert (Umberto Wolff until 1918) 45–46
women workers 25, 34–40, 43, 46–47, 65
    unemployment of 38–39, 43, 46–47
    see also Mary Macarthur Holiday Home(s); National Federation of Women Workers; National Union of General Workers; Queen Mary's Needlework Guild; Queen's Work for Women Fund; War Cabinet Committee on Women in Industry; Women's Trade Union League
Women's Trade Union League (WTUL) 25, 27, 34–40, 46, 64, 70
Woolwich Arsenal 36

X-rays in atomic research 83

Yokohama 48

Zanzibar 26
Zeppelin L31, shooting down of 29
Zutphen, Netherlands 89

www.ingramcontent.com/pod-product-compliance
Lightning Source LLC
LaVergne TN
LVHW041632070426
835507LV00008B/573